SAINT IGNATIUS LOYOLA

"But they that are learned, shall shine as the brightness of the firmament: and they that instruct many to justice, as stars for all eternity."
—Daniel 12:3

St. Ignatius greeting St. Francis Borgia
on his arrival in Rome.

SAINT IGNATIUS LOYOLA

1491-1556

FOUNDER OF THE JESUITS

By

F. A. Forbes

"For what doth it profit a man, if he gain the whole world, and suffer the loss of his own soul? Or what exchange shall a man give for his soul?" —Matthew 16:26

TAN BOOKS AND PUBLISHERS, INC.
Rockford, Illinois 61105

Nihil Obstat: John N. Strassmaier, S.J.
             Censor Deputatus

Imprimatur: Edmund Canon Surmont
             Vicar General
             Westminster
             August 1, 1913

Published in 1919 by R. & T. Washbourne, Limited, London, as *The Life of Saint Ignatius Loyola* in the series *Standard-bearers of the Faith: A Series of Lives of the Saints for Young and Old*. This edition is taken from the Third Edition.

ISBN 0-89555-624-3

Library of Congress Catalog Card No.: 98-61411

Cover illustration: Statue at the Shrine of Loyola: the young Ignatius as he surrenders himself to God. Photo by arrangement with Ediciones Beascoa S.A., Barcelona.

Printed and bound in the United States of America.

TAN BOOKS AND PUBLISHERS, INC.
P.O. Box 424
Rockford, Illinois 61105
1998

A PRAYER OF ST. IGNATIUS

DEAREST LORD, teach me to be generous. Teach me to serve Thee as Thou deservest: to give and not to count the cost; to fight and not to heed the wounds; to toil and not to seek for rest; to labor and not to seek reward, save that of knowing that I do Thy Will, O God.

CONTENTS

1. Pamplona—And After 1
2. The Battlefield 8
3. The Forging of the Weapons 14
4. Jerusalem 21
5. In the King's Service 29
6. The "Free Company" 36
7. The Warfare 46
8. The General and His Army 55
9. "Ad Majorem Dei Gloriam" 67
10. The Last Fight 75
11. The Legacy 85

INTRODUCTION

We know with what enthusiasm children read and ponder over the lives of those whose characters and deeds have won their admiration. They have even a way of identifying themselves with the personalities of their heroes and of repeating in imagination their achievements; nor is it so infrequent for this early cultivation of ideals to exercise a determining influence on the shaping of their after lives. It is thus, in fact, that in no small measure the great men and women of a nation are fashioned to their future calling.

Very similar, in the spiritual sphere, is the influence exercised on young people religiously brought up by the Lives of the Saints. Catholic children are particularly fond of this kind of reading. They realize vividly that the Saints are now reigning in Heaven and can watch over them and guide them just as, in accord with the words of the Psalmist, do their Guardian Angels. Hence they make them their mental companions, put trust in their intercessions, seek to assimilate their special spirit, cherish their favorite maxims and strive in their humbler way to imitate some of their actions. Children are not all alike, and save for a few chosen souls, their imitation necessarily falls far short of the pattern set. Still the practice is at all times elevating and sustaining, and it is a powerful instrument for their spiritual education.

But that Lives of the Saints may appeal thus to the young, they must be written in a special style. They must not be too complex or subjective, and even the attempt to be complete in giving all the facts and tracing analytically the growth of purpose and achievement may be overdone. What young people like best, and what is best for them, is to have the human interest and spiritual beauty of the Saint's life brought out in their relation to a succession of its most salient incidents, these being told in simple but pictorial language. It is on these principles that the short lives which are to form the present series have been undertaken by a writer who knows the tastes of Catholic youth.

The life which stands at the head of the projected list and occupies these pages is one that lends itself well to this mode of treatment. For it is the life of the soldier saint who, through meditation on the life of his Divine Master, was led to exchange an earthly for a heavenly warfare and who became, in Newman's words, the

"St. George of modern history," the Father of a long line of spiritual posterity whose zeal in the Church's service is acknowledged and whose methods and motives, though often misunderstood, are conformed to the pattern of their Founder.

—Sydney F. Smith, S.J.
September, 1913

SAINT IGNATIUS LOYOLA

"Amen I say to you, there is no man who hath left house or brethren, or sisters, or father, or mother, or children, or lands, for my sake and for the gospel, who shall not receive an hundred times as much, now in this time; houses, and brethren, and sisters, and mothers, and children, and lands, with persecutions: and in the world to come life everlasting."

—Mark 10:29-30

Chapter 1

PAMPLONA—AND AFTER

THE gray morning was breaking mistily over the little town of Pamplona in Navarre. To many of those within the citadel it seemed as if the grayness of the morning had found its way into their very hearts, so unpromising was the outlook that lay before them. The little garrison had been weakened by the retreat of many of the Spanish officers, their fortifications were incomplete, ammunition was scarce, and encamped at their very gates lay the French army. The attack might begin at any moment, and unless the expected reinforcements arrived, nothing could save the citadel.*

The idea of surrender had suggested itself to

---

*Note: In the year 1512 Navarre was annexed by Ferdinand of Spain. Nine years later Jean d'Albret, the rightful heir, assisted by the French, made an attempt to regain it. The sympathies of the Navarrese were entirely with the invading army, which advanced without hindrance to the walls of Pamplona, the capital, which had been hurriedly and partially fortified by the Spaniards. The French made their entrance into the citadel on May 20, 1521.

many minds and would certainly have been put into execution had it not been for the efforts of a young Spanish officer, Iñigo or Ignatius de Loyola. For days he had been exhorting the weak, encouraging the fainthearted and putting something of his own high courage and hopefulness into every heart.

The Viceroy would certainly come to their relief, he urged; the conditions offered by the French were most humiliating to the Spanish pride. For the honor of their country, let them hold out a little longer and all would be well.

It was hardly to be wondered at that young Loyola, endowed as he was with a marvelous gift of influencing others, was the darling of his men and a favorite with all. His family was one of the noblest in Spain; he had already distinguished himself on the field of battle, but it was not only as a soldier that he excelled. An expert in all the manly sports of the time, he could write a love sonnet or a religious poem with equal ease and illuminate them skillfully when written. He was a good dancer in a country where men and women are born with rhythm and music in their feet. But he was above and beyond all these things a man of war. His dearest aspiration was to win honor and glory as a soldier— to make for himself a name which should live in the history of his country.

We shall see later how this aspiration was realized, but the battlefield and the manner of the warfare were hidden for the present in the secret counsels of God.

Ignatius' hope of a speedy reinforcement was vain. The Viceroy did not come, and the attack began that day. The assault was desperate, but the young Spaniard fought like a hero of old. Wherever the fire was hottest he was to be seen on the ramparts, a figure in shining armor, fighting with the strength of ten. Assailant after assailant fell dead at his feet or was hurled backwards over the ramparts, but the citadel was doomed. A cannonball struck the battlements where Loyola stood, sword in hand, like a young Achilles, and rebounded, shattering his right leg and grazing the left. Ignatius fell, and with him fell Pamplona.

When the wounded man recovered consciousness, he was lying in a tent in the French camp, and one of the most distinguished of the French officers sat beside his bed. Slowly the truth began to dawn on Ignatius' weary brain: he was a prisoner, and Pamplona was taken. Then his eyes fell upon his sword, and he began to wonder.

"I am your prisoner," he said, turning to the Frenchman, "and yet they have left me my arms."

The officer bowed with a chivalrous courtesy.

"All brave men can appreciate true valor, Don Iñigo," he replied. "You are our guest; is there anything that I can do for you? I am at your service."

The young Spaniard thought for a moment.

"My uncle, the Duke of Najera, is on his way to Pamplona," he replied. "I should be grateful if you would let him know that I did my best."

As soon as he was able to bear the journey, Ignatius was conveyed to the castle of Loyola, where he was received by his elder brother, Don Martin. There the leg, owing to the unskillful setting of the bone, had to be broken afresh, and for several days his life was in danger.

Long weeks of weary suffering followed, not the least part of which, to the active spirit of the young soldier, was the enforced inaction, for every movement caused him pain. At last the wound healed and the doctors examined the injured leg carefully.

There was just one thing they thought perhaps they ought to mention. The right leg would be a trifle shorter than the left, and a little less shapely. The vanity of the invalid took alarm. Owing to the dress of the period, with its long, tightly fitting hose, any peculiarity in gait was very noticeable. Ignatius was not a little proud of his good looks and his graceful carriage.

Was there no remedy, he asked anxiously;

could nothing be done?

The doctors looked at each other gravely.

There was one remedy, they said, but they would hardly advise it. The wound would have to be reopened, part of the bone sawed off, and the leg stretched with an iron machine—then possibly all might be well.

"Do it," replied Ignatius promptly.

The doctors still hesitated. The operation would be a very painful one, they objected, and would be followed by many weeks of suffering during which the patient would have to remain perfectly still.

"Do it," repeated Ignatius doggedly.

In those days the modern inventions for deadening pain were unknown. The patient was firmly tied down and, fully conscious of all that was going on, endured as best he might. Ignatius, like the gallant soldier he was, set his teeth and bore the pain without flinching. But when all was over, and the anguish of the tortured limb was a little easier, the thought of the weary days before him was almost more than he could bear.

"Bring me a book, a story, a novel, anything to pass away the time!" he cried. Books were scarce in the castle of Loyola, for printing had but lately been invented. They brought him what they had, and Ignatius read.

Now the things that happen on this earth

seem often to fall out by chance, and men are apt to forget that the will of God is behind them, ordering and directing all. One of the books that fell into Ignatius' hands was a story that has ever moved the hearts of men to the noblest thoughts and actions. It was the *Life of Christ*, written by a Carthusian monk of Saxony, who had brought to his task a mind enlightened by the loving study of the Scriptures and a heart purified by long hours of prayer.

The heart of the young soldier flamed within him as he read. Surely here was the Master of whom he had always dreamed, a hero-king whom it would be indeed an honor to serve; a leader of men, whom it would be truly worthwhile to follow. He prayed as he lay on his bed of suffering and learned to make a friend of the Lord whom he was beginning to know. In spirit he followed Him through the towns and cities of Galilee, rejoicing, as a heart that has at last found its ideal, in His noble and gracious presence. It was to be a lifelong friendship for Ignatius, and one that was to grow in strength as the years rolled on.

But the change was not effected in a moment. The daydreams of his early life came back persistently. Why should he give up all that was so attractive to his youth and ambition? For to take service under this new Master meant the renunciation of all that was pleasant to nature. What would his friends say? Would they not laugh at him at court? But the voice of the Divine Leader sounded above the tumult of the flesh, calling the young Loyola to His service.

One night when the desire to do what was best was strong in his soul, prostrating himself before a statue of the Blessed Virgin he bound himself in true soldier's language to follow her Divine Son to the death. At that moment a shock like that of an earthquake shook the castle of Loyola, breaking the windows and cracking the wall of his room from top to bottom.

Chapter 2

THE BATTLEFIELD

"THE Gates of Hell shall not prevail against it," said Our Lord, speaking of His kingdom—that Church of His which He had come on earth to found. He did not say that the Gates of Hell should not fight against it; He knew, on the contrary, how bitter the warfare was to be, and how unceasing. He knew that it was a warfare that would last while the world lasted, and that sometimes the hearts of His faithful would sink within them, while they asked themselves, as the Apostles had done before them, whether their Lord and Master were not asleep, that He seemed to take so little heed of the storm that was raging round them.

There were to be the enemies from without —did not Our Lord Himself foretell it? "You shall be hated by all men for My name's sake." But more bitter still, there were to be the enemies from within. It could not be otherwise. While the world lasted, human nature would be human nature still, with its possibilities for good or evil; and many would leave the good and choose the evil—the pleasanter because the easier course. Of the twelve Apostles, one was a traitor—one that had lived in the very presence of the Son of God and heard with his own ears the teaching that was to draw men's souls to Heaven. Could it be otherwise with the Church of Christ? Was it meant to be otherwise? The wheat and the tares were to grow together, said the Master, till the harvest, and the harvest was the end of the world.

Through all the centuries we see it still the same—the powers of good and evil fighting even within the Church, the cockle and the wheat growing side by side. Among the wise and strong, the Saints and martyrs who have sat on the throne of Peter, there have been wicked men, imbued with a worldly spirit. "Have I not chosen you twelve, and one of you is a devil?" It is the unfaithful children of the Church that have inflicted on her the cruelest wounds— "mine own familiar friend in whom I trusted; if it had been another I could have borne it."

Yet stands the promise, and the promise shall not fail. The Gates of Hell shall not prevail against the Church of Christ. He will be with her all days even to the end of the world; and, as a mighty king sends forth his generals to fight against his foes, so has Our Lord raised up to

Himself in all ages mighty champions to fight for His truth.

St. Augustine of Hippo, who stands with St. Mary Magdalene at the head of the army of the glorious penitents of Christ, was the chosen champion of the Church in Africa. "Too late have I loved Thee, O Beauty ever ancient and ever new!" was the cry of his heart, as he labored with all the strength of his great soul against his Master's enemies.

When the corruption of the Rome of the Caesars had distilled its poison throughout the civilized countries of Europe, and even the clergy were not untainted by the vices which they were powerless to check, Benedict, a young Roman patrician, fled from that world where self-indulgence reigned supreme to found in prayer, labor and self-denial that order which was to be the regenerating force of the centuries which followed.

Later, when the world was growing cold again under the passion for pomp and splendor which was such a characteristic of the Middle Ages, Francis, the Poor Man of Assisi, went out from his father's home to preach the love of poverty, drawing multitudes to forsake their sinful lives and follow that Master of whom he was so attractive a representative.

While St. Francis was preaching in the mountains of Umbria, St. Dominic was founding his Order of Preachers—"the dogs of the Lord"— who were to stand so staunchly by the Church of Christ, able defenders of truth and teachers of doctrine.

With the Renaissance a new danger had arisen. The revival of learning was an excellent thing in its way; but like many other excellent things, it had its drawbacks. In the first place let us understand that the word "learning," when used in connection with the Renaissance, meant one branch of learning only—the study of classical authors and of classical art. Now the ancient writers of Greece and Rome were pagans, and they lived for the most part in an age when the corruption of the civilized world was proverbial. They wrote for a corrupt age, and side by side with great and noble thoughts is much that appeals only to the basest and lowest in man.

The rage for everything that was classical became a passion in Southern Europe and spread even to the Northern countries. No one was esteemed of any worth unless he was a good Greek and Latin scholar; and if he were a "humanist," it did not matter how evil a life he might lead or how shameful his writings might be— he was everywhere courted and admired.

So the pagan spirit crept in with the pagan authors. The tales of heathen gods and goddesses were read more eagerly than the lives of the Saints or their writings—Ovid and Horace were preferred to the Holy Scriptures. The poison spread through all classes. Many of the clergy took the infection. Faith had grown dim; fervor had relaxed; splendor and luxury reigned supreme; and that fatal love of pleasure and unbridled self-indulgence that had dragged the world down so many times before was dragging it down again. The Venus of Titian had taken the place of the Madonnas of Fra Angelico.

There was need of reform. No one saw it more clearly than the Church herself, as the writings and lives of the holy men of the time bear witness. But where the reform was needed was in the lives and morals of the clergy and the people, in the more faithful following of that noble ideal which the Church of Christ sets and has always set before her children—not in the pulling down of that ideal to a lower level, nor in the assailing of those doctrines of which Christ has made His holy Church the guardian.

Not so thought Martin Luther, an Augustinian monk of Saxony who, casting off the restraints of the monastic life with his monk's habit, had married an apostate nun, attacked openly nearly every dogma of the Catholic Church and was preaching his own doctrine throughout Germany.

The easygoing took readily to the new teaching. Luther's doctrine of "justification by faith" was essentially a comfortable one, doing away as it did with all necessity for penance and mortification. "Believe, and take it easy," is a morepleasant maxim for flesh and blood than "Deny thyself, and take up the Cross." The tide of an advancing Protestantism could only have been checked by devoted self-sacrifice, noble endeavor and purity of life among the clergy. Alas, the poison of the Renaissance had done its work too well! Its pagan teaching had stolen away from many their manliness and their strength.

"Lord, is it nothing to Thee that we perish?" went up, as of old, the cry of God's people. The storm raged pitilessly indeed round the bark of Peter. . . .

His promise shall not fail. . . .

On the threshold of the castle of Loyola stood Ignatius, the soldier, the champion of Christ; and the words of another great Saint, whose conversion was as marvelous as his own, were on his lips.

"Lord, what wilt Thou have me to do?"

The answer was not long to be withheld.

Chapter 3

THE FORGING OF THE WEAPONS

A DAY'S journey inland from Barcelona, where the blue waters of the Mediterranean bathe the sunny coast of Spain, stands a tall and rugged mountain whose peaks are shaped like the sharp edge of a saw. Montserrat, or "the saw mountain," it is called by the Spaniards; and on its rocky flanks stands one of the most famous shrines of the Madonna, "Our Lady of Montserrat." The sunset of an early spring evening was tinging the sharp peaks with crimson as a lonely cavalier rode slowly up the steep mountain road that leads to the sanctuary. The lonely rider was Ignatius.

Whither was he bound, this young knight errant? The answer was not yet clear to himself. Dreams of the Holy Land filled his thoughts, for in Spain, even in the times of which we write, "Crusade" was still a word to make every noble heart leap. Was that his Master's will for him? Ignatius could not tell. Soldier-like he awaited the word of command, ready for whatever was to come.

In the meantime he felt the need of solitude, of penance and of prayer. That ardent nature was not one to do things by halves. On the mountain road he met a beggar and, bestowing on him his rich garments of silk and velvet, clothed himself in a long tunic of sackcloth and girt it round him with a rope. Thus clad, in the dusk of the evening, he hung up his sword and dagger over Our Lady's altar and, like a true knight, prepared to keep his vigil of arms. It was the eve of the Annunciation, 1522.

The evening shadows lengthened into night, the moonbeams crept through the tall arched windows of the chapel, making strange patterns on floor and wall and playing about the motionless figure that knelt with outstretched arms before the shrine. All through the hours of darkness Ignatius watched in prayer, offering himself to the will of his "liege Lord," promising to be His "man" and to fight His battles forever. It was the dedication of the new life.

At daybreak, after having heard Mass and received his Lord, he went his way to the little town of Manresa, not far distant. Taking shelter there in the hospital of St. Lucy, he undertook to tend the sick, choosing out the most ill-natured and those who were suffering from the most loathsome diseases. He would gather the little children of the streets around him and teach them their catechism. All his leisure time was spent in prayer. Under the sackcloth gown he wore a sharp girdle or cincture of iron, and a hairshirt took the place of the fine linen in which he had used to delight.

Men stared and questioned; there was something in the noble bearing of the young stranger, in the flash of his keen dark eyes, altogether out of keeping with the sackcloth gown. "He is a prince in disguise," they whispered. Others jeered at him as a fool. Neither the sackcloth nor the penance came easily to Ignatius. More than once in the hospital his nature revolted against the sights, the smells, the work he had set himself to do; and the temptation to leave it all, to return to the old life where everything had been so pleasant to the senses, came strongly upon him. He met it with the old soldier spirit and, seeking out those who were suffering from cancer or leprosy or other repulsive diseases, kissed their sores, washing and dressing them with redoubled tenderness.

Thus passed several months, but Ignatius was not yet satisfied. In the rocky hillside near Manresa was a cave, the entrance of which was overgrown with briars and bushes. In this cave he determined to take up his abode. With no bed but the hard ground, with no light but that which filtered through the small opening by which he had entered, he prayed and did penance, asking counsel of God. There he learned that he was to found an order, and that the order was to be for the saving of men's souls.

It was hardly to be expected that the enemy of mankind should leave in peace one who was destined to snatch so many from his grasp. The assaults of the evil one were frequent and strong. Temptations to give up everything and to return to the old life; temptations to despair; temptations to pride; and, worst of all, agonies of scruples, succeeded each other with scarcely a break.

Against each one the brave soldier spirit fought to the last, and after ten months of sore battle came peace and light. Throughout his life there remained with Ignatius, as the fruit of these weeks of suffering, a special gift of helping and consoling those in temptation or in trial. In the cave of Manresa, too, in prayer and conflict, was forged that weapon which was to be such a powerful instrument against the enemy of souls— *The Spiritual Exercises of St. Ignatius.*

The Exercises which, it is said, have won more souls to God than there are letters in the book, consist of a series of meditations, intended originally to extend over a period of four weeks, but which can be shortened at will to a week or even less.

Now meditation is a long word which describes a very simple thing, and one which consciously or unconsciously nearly all of us spend a great part of our lives in doing. Ignatius on his sickbed at Loyola would probably have been as much alarmed at the idea of making a meditation as many another young man of his age. Yet, as he lay reading the *Life of Christ*, musing afterward on what he had read, picturing to himself the Master as He went about doing good, humbly asking forgiveness of his sins and grace to serve that Master better, he was making unconsciously a very good meditation indeed.

He who makes the Exercises—or an "Ignation retreat" as we call it nowadays—is required to put away for the time all thought of outside things and, as far as possible, in silence and solitude, to make the meditations as they are given. The exercises are, to put it shortly, the teaching of the Gospel driven home. In the meditations of the first week, the great truth that God has made man to serve and praise Him, and given him the world and all that is in it for this purpose, is first proposed. Then sin, the certainty of death for all and the life to come—Hell or Heaven—are to be considered, together with the infinite mercy of God and His tenderness to repentant sinners. In the second week the "retreatant" meditates on the life of Our Lord as it is shown in the Gospel.

There, in the stable at Bethlehem, in the carpenter's shop at Nazareth, in the villages and towns of Judea, he learns to love and imitate his Lord who came down from Heaven to take our humanity upon Him and to teach us the way of Life. In the meditation on the Kingdom of Christ he asks himself, as Ignatius had asked himself at Loyola, if such a leader and King is not worth the whole-hearted devotion of His subjects, and he resolves from henceforth to be His faithful disciple and follower.

In the third week he meditates on the bitter Passion and death of Christ, remembering that they were endured for his salvation. Since his Lord has suffered so much for him, can he not bear in his turn a little of the hardships of life, of self-denial and self-control for Him? "This have I done for thee, what doest thou for Me?" asks the Christ, and the heart of the weakest takes courage.

The fourth week is occupied with the thought of Heaven and the eternal happiness that awaits those who have followed their Master faithfully on earth. There the retreatant sees how "the sufferings of this earth, which are but for a moment, are not worthy to be compared with the glory that shall be revealed in us," and, confronted by the shining army of the Saints of God who have overcome, he asks their help to persevere in the fight that is before him, that he too may one day rejoice with them in glory.

In the lonely cave at Manresa the stone is still shown on which Ignatius wrote the plan of the exercises and over which the vision of the Blessed Mother of God is said to have hovered, inspiring and counseling him as he wrote. It is all so simple, and yet so wonderful in its effects, that later on men who saw the changed lives of those who had made the Exercises would ask themselves what sorcery or magic Ignatius and his followers had employed.

"Did they show you devils and witches?" asked the awe-stricken young friend of one who came out of his "retreat" a changed man.

"Much worse," answered he; "they showed me myself."

This is the end and the work of the Exercises. "Lord, let me know Thee and know myself, that I may love Thee and hate myself," St. Augustine was used to pray. In these two things lies the seed of holiness.

Chapter 4

JERUSALEM

IN the loneliness and silence of Manresa, Ignatius had learned to wield the sword of the spirit as manfully as he had ever used the strong blade that still hung by Our Lady's altar at Montserrat. He had conquered self and had beaten off the enemy at every point. He had learned the science of the Christian warfare, but his heart still ached with a desire that was now at last to find its fulfillment. Taking palmer's staff in hand, barefooted and begging his bread by the way, Ignatius set forth on pilgrimage to Jerusalem to venerate the holy places that had been blessed by the earthly presence of his Lord.

The first stage in his journey was Barcelona. It was Lent, and a famous preacher was drawing crowds to his sermons in the cathedral. Ignatius entered and, taking his place among the children on the altar steps—for the church was overflowing—listened with reverent attention to the words of the priest. The sight of the stranger in pilgrim garb, sitting thus humbly in his lowly place, made a profound impression on a lady who was present, Doña Isabel Roser.

There was something noble and at the same time strangely suggestive of Heaven in the face that was before her; a supernatural light seemed to play about the head of the pilgrim. On reaching home she spoke of him to her husband, who at once sent a servant to seek out the stranger and ask him to come and pay them a visit. Ignatius was still in the cathedral, and he assented courteously to the request.

So sweetly and eloquently did he speak to them of the things of God, that they were loath to let him go and earnestly entreated him to make his home with them until he left Barcelona. This, however, he gently refused to do. He had resolved, he said, to stay at the hospital and devote his time to the care of the sick. Then they besought him to let them pay for his journey; but again he answered that he meant to beg a passage for the love of God and, when he reached land, to pursue his travels on foot.

In a few days he set sail, and, reaching Gaeta, set out for Rome. But he was a sorry pedestrian; the wounded leg, not yet quite sound, caused him intense pain, and the bread for which he begged was sometimes not forthcoming. The plague was raging in Italy, and the pale and haggard face of the pilgrim frightened the country people, who, fearing that he was attacked by the disease, would hardly let him into their towns or villages. At last, after many trials, footsore and weary, hungry and exhausted, he came in sight of the Eternal City seated on its seven hills.

The very sight of Rome refreshed his weary spirit; the earth his feet were treading had been watered by the blood of the martyrs; everything that met his eyes reminded him of the hero saints of old. It was Holy Week, and he resolved to remain in Rome till after Easter, to pray at the tombs of St. Peter and St. Paul and of all the glorious company of the Blessed that lie within that hallowed spot of ground. Then, fortified by the blessing of the Pope, and armed with his pilgrim's licence for Jerusalem, he set forth on his way to Venice.

Fresh misfortunes awaited him. Once more his pallor and weakness so alarmed the people that they fled from him in terror, again believing him to be plague-stricken; and once more the pilgrim toiled on his way, shunned and avoided by all. He entered Venice by night and, utterly exhausted, lay down to sleep on the ground under the portico of the palace of Marc Antonio Trevisano, a future Doge of Venice. In the silence of the night a voice spoke to the noble Senator, saying, "Sleepest thou comfortably in thy rich bed, while My faithful servant lies near thee on the stones?" The Venetian went forth with servants and torches, and all but stumbled over the body of Ignatius, too weary to move.

He was at once brought into the palace and tended with the greatest care. Trevisano would have liked to keep his holy guest, but Ignatius, ever a lover of poverty, was unhappy in his rich surroundings.

On July 14 he set sail in the vessel that was bearing the Governor General to Cyprus, having missed the pilgrims' ship which had started a few days before. But the conversation and the conduct of the passengers, and still more that of the crew, filled the Saint with grief and indignation.

Earnestly he exhorted them to turn to God and amend their lives, but the only effect of his words was to rouse their pride and anger. At last they resolved to cast him ashore on a desert rock in the Mediterranean, where the horrors of a slow starvation would silence forever the voice that had tried to awaken their sleeping souls. Ignatius, aware of their project, commended himself to God and prayed. The Almighty was watching over His servant; a violent wind arose which beat the ship to the port of Famagosta in Cyprus. Crossing the island, Ignatius found the pilgrims' ship, which he had missed at Venice, about to sail for Jaffa. Well had he said when he set forth on his pilgrimage, "I am under the protection of the King of Heaven and of earth, whose servant I am; it suffices me, for it will never fail."

At the end of August, seven months after his departure from Manresa, he set foot in that Holy Land which had been indeed the country of his dreams. The pilgrims entered the Holy City in procession and in profound silence; in their hearts, perhaps, was the thought of the first Crusaders, walking thus two and two, barefoot and bareheaded, their rich robes laid aside out of reverence for One who was poor and in sorrows from His youth.

"Jerusalem, Jerusalem, how often would I have gathered thy children together as the hen doth gather her chickens under her wings, and thou wouldst not. Behold your house shall be left to you desolate." Desolate indeed she appeared to the little band of pilgrims, scarcely the shadow of that Jerusalem of old, the beautiful "City of Peace." She had done penance for her sins; the armies of Rome had razed her to the foundations; war and famine and pestilence had raged within her walls; even now a heathen power held her captive, and yet—she was still the Jerusalem of Christ, loved of all men for His Name's sake; her very stones were sweet with His memory.

Who shall say what heavenly graces were

received by Ignatius as he knelt prostrate on the
ground, washing with his tears that earth that
had been touched by the feet of his Redeemer?
Again and again he visited the spots made sacred
by the presence of Christ, kissing with adoring
love the place of his Lord's agony and crucifix-
ion.

For years Jerusalem had been the hope of his
heart; at Jerusalem he would gladly have
remained, but this was not to be, for Palestine
was not destined to be the home of his order.
The battlefield of the Company of Jesus was to
be the whole world. But this Ignatius did not
then know. He went to the Superior of the Franciscans and asked leave to remain in the Holy
City to work for the conversion of the heathen.

The Provincial was absent, they told him, and
no one else could give the required permission.
He was at Bethlehem, but they expected him
back in a few days and would then place Ignatius'
request before him. The absence of the Father
Provincial, however, was longer than had been
foreseen; it was not until two months after his
arrival in the Holy Land that Ignatius obtained
the desired interview. The Provincial was kind
but firm. He thoroughly approved of the Saint's
devotion, but after careful consideration of the
question, he decided that it would be best for
him to leave Jerusalem with the other pilgrims.

The monastery was poor; it was all they could do to support themselves. Moreover, it was no uncommon thing for Christians to be killed by the Turks or sold into slavery; the risks would be too great. In vain Ignatius protested that he would beg his bread and be no expense to the friars, that he feared neither slavery nor death— the Franciscan was not to be moved. So ardent and zealous a nature as the Spaniard's, he said, would never be able to submit to the rules imposed by the Turkish authorities, obedience to which was the condition of their being allowed to remain. The danger would be too great, for Ignatius himself as well as for the Franciscans. Moreover, the Pope had given authority to the Provincial to decide in such cases who was to remain and who was not; his decision was to be considered final. To this last argument Ignatius submitted at once; he was ready, he said, to obey. He made his preparations for departure, but he was to justify, to a certain extent, the fears of the good Franciscan before he left the Holy City.

A longing came over him to visit once more the footprints of the Saviour on the mount of the Ascension, and, desiring to be alone that he might have the more leisure for prayer, he set off without the Turkish escort that was of obligation for all pilgrims. For a Christian to venture alone outside the walls of the city was a rash and dangerous undertaking, but Ignatius cared little for this. He reached the summit of the hill without hindrance, but there he was stopped by the Moslem guards who kept the mosque built over the sacred spot.

He gained admittance by bribing one of them with his penknife, and having satisfied his devotion, turned to retrace his steps toward Jerusalem. But he had not gone far before it struck him that he had not noticed in what direction the sacred footsteps pointed.

Back he went again, this time offering a pair of scissors, his last belonging, to the conveniently indulgent guard.

Meanwhile he had been missed by the Franciscans who, fearing lest he might have gotten into difficulties with the Turks, sent out an Armenian servant to search for the wanderer. The Armenian, angry at the pilgrim's adventure, perhaps because it interrupted his own work, abused him roundly and even threatened him with his stick. Then seizing him roughly by the arm, he dragged him back to the convent, rating him soundly all the way. Ignatius heeded neither the insults nor the rough usage. Before him stood Our Lord Himself as He had appeared to the disciples on the mount of the Ascension, and the heart of His servant was filled with consolation.

Chapter 5

IN THE KING'S SERVICE

SORROWFULLY, yet not sorrowfully, since God's ways are always best, our pilgrim turned his back on the land of his desires and set out for Spain. The hope still remained in his heart that some day in the future he would be allowed to return to work for souls in Palestine. At Cyprus he begged a free passage on a Venetian ship that was about to sail, but the captain refused him rudely. "He asks a passage for the love of God; let him walk on the water for the love of God," said he, "for no passage shall he get from me."

Alongside lay a Turkish ship, which also refused the Saint's petition; he then turned to a crazy little bark, bound likewise for Venice, the captain of which bade him come on board at once. Next day the three vessels put out to sea.

The Turkish ship perished with all hands on board; the fine Italian boat stranded off the coast of Cyprus, narrowly escaping shipwreck. The miserable craft that had given Ignatius passage, alone of the three, made its way safely through storms to Venice, having taken two months for the voyage.

Then followed a long journey on foot. France and Spain were at war. Our pilgrim, after falling first into the hands of the Spaniards, who took him for a spy, and then into those of the French, by whom he was better treated than by his own countrymen, at last reached Genoa, where he embarked for Barcelona.

It was the spring of 1524. Ignatius had been thinking deeply, and the work of the immediate future lay definitely before him. More than once already the misgiving had crossed his mind that his own lack of education might form a serious obstacle to the Master's work, for he was no scholar. The new learning had not been in vogue among young men of fashion in the days of his boyhood, and the lively and unruly disposition of the young Iñigo had made it a harder thing than usual to keep him to his books. Courtesy and knightly honor he had learned as a page in the court of Ferdinand the Catholic; under his uncle the Duke of Najera he had studied the art of war; but Greek and Latin had formed part of the program in neither court nor camp.

With the determined will that went straight at every obstacle and overcame it, this man of thirty-three resolved to begin his education at the very beginning. At Barcelona he found a schoolmaster and, taking his place on the school benches among children and half-grown lads, set himself to the task before him.

For two years he labored at verbs and declensions, living meanwhile in a room lent him by the charity of Doña Ines Pascual. Up to the door of this room at night would creep Juan, the young son of Doña Ines, to peep awe-stricken through the keyhole at the Saint, who spent most of the night in prayer and was often to be seen, the boy declared, surrounded by a strange and beautiful light. He begged his daily bread, and since on account of the veneration in which he was held by the good people of Barcelona he had always more than he could use, the best of everything was given to the poor. Doña Ines used often to object to this arrangement, but her holy guest would answer, "Señora, if Our Lord Jesus Christ were to ask you for an alms, would you give Him the worst of what you had?"

Nor did Ignatius confine his apostleship to the poor alone. Many young men who were leading bad lives were won over by his gentle persuasiveness to nobler and better things.

The two years at Barcelona at last drew to a close. At the University of Alcalá, owing to the charity of its noble founder, Cardinal Ximenes, provision had been made for the training of poor scholars. Thither Ignatius was advised to go, and thither he went in the beginning of August 1526. Here also he determined to beg for what he needed for himself and his poor, for wherever he went the poor were wont to hail him as a friend raised up to them by God. The needs of the sick in the hospitals, of the children in the streets, of the young men in the schools, appealed irresistibly to his apostolic zeal.

The bad life of a certain young ecclesiastic was scandalizing the town. Ignatius went to visit him and gently but firmly showed him the harm he was doing to himself and to others. For answer the angry young man threatened to throw his unwelcome guest out the window. Ignatius, with his usual winning charity, persisted, and in the end prevailed. The Exercises were made, and a changed life was the result. This sudden and complete conversion caused a nine days' wonder in Alcalá. The young students flocked round Ignatius begging for help and advice, and his extraordinary influence was talked of everywhere.

The authorities began to be suspicious. Who was this student, they asked, whose power over others was such that sorcery or magic had been suggested as the only explanation? Here was a man who had come to learn and was taking upon himself to teach. A secret disciple of Luther, probably, if not worse. It would be well to be careful. Strange rumors even reached the headquarters of the Inquisition at Toledo, and Don Juan de Figueroa, the Vicar General at Alcalá, was asked to investigate the matter. The climax came in a complaint from a person of influence in the town that two ladies under his guardianship had gone alone on a dangerous pilgrimage without his consent. He was certain that it was by Ignatius' direction.

Loyola was seized and carried off to prison. On the way the poor beggar-student and his custodians had to stand aside to let pass the imposing cortège of the grandees of Alcalá, who were doing the honors of the town to the young Marquis of Lombay, a boy of seventeen. The eyes of the prisoner and those of the Marquis met, as Ignatius courteously doffed his cap. Little did the boy dream that the poor beggar before him was one day to be the General of the Society of Jesus, and his own father in Christ, for the Marquis of Lombay was none other than Francis Borgia.

In prison Ignatius was visited by Figueroa, who treated him kindly.

"If you could only do things like other people," he said, "it would be all right. But you go in for such novelties."

"Could you call it a novelty, my lord, to speak

of Christ to Christians?" replied Ignatius.

In all things he said he was ready to submit himself to the Church; if his doctrines were unorthodox, let them be condemned.

He was set free and completely absolved from all blame, but he was not to preach till his four years of study were completed.

Ignatius' mission at Alcalá was at an end. He went to seek advice of the Archbishop of Toledo, who counselled him to go to the University of Salamanca where he could continue his studies and his apostolate together. To Salamanca therefore he went, but only to find that his fame had preceded him. He had not been there a fortnight before he was cited to appear before the authorities.

Why did he preach, and on what subjects?

He preached on virtue and vice, was the answer, to induce men to practice the one and avoid the other.

How could he speak of such things without being learned?

The matter was laid before the Grand Vicar, who demanded that all papers, particularly the Exercises, should be delivered into his hands, Ignatius declaring as usual that he was ready to submit himself to rightful authority. A formal examination took place, and Ignatius answered subtle theological questions with a directness and skill that astonished his examiners.

"Preach," they said, "and let us hear how you do it—speak to us on the First Commandment."

Ignatius spoke with his usual fire and eloquence. The judges listened enraptured. There could be no doubt of the sincerity of such a man.

They were satisfied at all points, they said, but it would be better not to speak on certain subjects until the four years' course was finished.

The prohibition meant complete silence. Ignatius resolved to depart. Spain with her formalism and conservatism was not destined to be the birthplace of the Society of Jesus.

Alone Ignatius set out for Paris. The little band of disciples who had gathered round him at Alcalá were to remain behind and continue their studies. Did Ignatius know that once the presence of their master was withdrawn, not one of them was to persevere? It was not long before they began to ask themselves if the life they had undertaken was not beyond their strength. Theirs was the comfortable humility of Sir Gawain when the quest of the Holy Grail was proposed, with all its dangers and hardships, to the knights of Arthur's court.

"This quest is not for me," they said, and dropped off one by one, to find some easier road to Heaven.

Chapter 6

THE "FREE COMPANY"

AMONG the students who came flocking to the University of Paris in the sixteenth century were men of all classes and of all nations. The beggar student brushed elbows with the young nobleman—the Spaniard sat down with the Greek. Ignatius had been prevailed upon by his friends in Spain to accept a small sum of money, sufficient to relieve him from the constant necessity of begging. In company with two or three poor students like himself he took a humble lodging, but the arrangement was to be of short duration. One of the young roommates suddenly disappeared, and Ignatius' money with him. He was thus forced to retire to the Hospital of St. James, where the poor were lodged free of cost.

Meanwhile his influence was already making itself felt. Three young Spanish students, after having gone through the Exercises, had sold all their possessions, given the proceeds to the poor and followed Ignatius to the hospital. The authorities were thoroughly irate, particularly the rectors of the colleges to which the young men belonged: Ortiz of Montaigu, and Gouvea of Ste. Barbe. They denounced Ignatius to the Inquisition as a heretic and a mischief-maker, adding that he had shown his guilt by flight.

A certain color was lent to this story by the fact that Ignatius was not to be found. The young man who had stolen his money had fallen ill on the way home and, friendless and in want, had written for help to the very man he had injured. Ignatius' vengeance was swift and saintlike. Barefoot and fasting, he set out in search of the prodigal, offering the hardships of the journey for the young man's soul. He found the thief both sick and sorry. With a mother's tenderness he nursed him back to health and sent him, healed in soul and body, to his home in Salamanca. Then, for the first time, he heard through a friend of the hue and cry in Paris.

Hastening back to the capital, he presented himself before the Grand Inquisitor, explained his conduct and begged him to let the trial take place as soon as possible, as the winter session was about to begin. The Inquisitor replied that a trial was unnecessary; he was completely satisfied.

The preliminary studies at Montaigu ended, Ignatius began his course of philosophy at Ste.

Barbe, under the rectorship of the very Gouvea who had but lately been so hot against him. He shared a room with Peter Favre (or Faber), a young Genevan, who had begun life as a shepherd boy on the Swiss mountains and whose brilliant intellectual gifts had brought him to Paris, where he had already taken his doctor's degree. He undertook to help Ignatius with his studies, and it was not long before the Spaniard realized that his young companion was destined to do great work in the world for God. Pure and holy in the midst of surroundings that were often neither the one nor the other, he needed only the spiritual guidance of Ignatius to bring out all that was latent in his sweet and noble nature.

In two years the young man was ordained a priest, after having gone through the Exercises under Ignatius' direction, who then confided to him his hopes for the future.

"I will follow you," said Favre, "through life and death."

Ignatius advised him to visit his parents and obtain their consent, but on his arrival at home he found that his mother was dead. His father had nothing to give him but his blessing, but Peter's desire was to be poor; he was thenceforward dependent on the alms which he and Ignatius obtained by begging. By nature humble and timid, Favre had yet to learn his own powers. At his master's bidding, he was ready to attempt difficult and dangerous enterprises and to dare all things to win souls to Christ.

Nor was Favre the only student of Ste. Barbe who succumbed to the charm of Ignatius. As usual the young men gathered round him, and the public disputations that were held on Sundays began soon to be forsaken for prayer and the reception of the Sacraments.

The professors complained to Gouvea, the rector, who lent them a sympathetic ear. A law existed by which unruly students could be flogged—it should be put in force at once. The needful steps were taken, and all preparations made. The news, however, reached the ears of a friend of Loyola, and he was at once warned of what was afoot.

The noble Spanish blood in Ignatius' veins boiled at the thought of the insult; no man who had undergone that ordeal could ever hope to hold up his head again—and yet— had not his Master borne worse things for him? The struggle was sharp but short. If his Lord would have it so—so let it be.

Down to the college with his own gentle dignity he went. Masters and students were gathered together in the great hall; all was in readiness. Ignatius asked to see the rector and was taken to him at once.

The minutes passed slowly by in a silence that could be felt; the crowds in the great hall held their breath.

At last the door opened, and judge and culprit entered together. But what was this?

The eyes of the angry Gouvea were wet with tears, and suddenly he knelt at the delinquent's feet. Before the whole assembly he humbly asked forgiveness of Ignatius and of God for the wrong that had been done to an innocent man.

The result of this strange scene was a complete reaction in favor of Ignatius, and for a time all went well. In March 1534 he took the degree of Master of Arts and came forth at the age of forty-four a scholar of the schools.

Among the young Spaniards at the University of Paris was one who looked with a certain contempt on the poor student whose name was on every lip. Of blood as noble as Ignatius' own, young Francis Xavier was as gifted as he was ambitious and was destined by his father for a brilliant career in the Church. Appointed, after only four years' study, lecturer at the college of Beauvais, the young professor was already charming all critics by his power and eloquence.

Coming out one evening from the college, elated with success and dreaming of the glorious career before him, his eyes fell on the unwelcome figure of the beggar student who stood in the shadow of the street watching him with dark, intent eyes. Annoyed at the meeting, Francis would have hurried by, but from out of the shadows spoke a voice low and distinct: "What doth it profit a man if he gain the whole world and suffer the loss of his own soul?"

If Xavier had been annoyed before, he was thoroughly angry now.

What had he and a beggar like Ignatius in common? He had no wish for his company nor his advice. The remark, moreover, was altogether wide of the mark. He had no intention of losing his soul, and as for gaining the world, well, the world and its honors were for those who deserved them.

So argued the young man resentfully, but the words of the poor student haunted his thoughts with an intolerable persistency. At night they would shine out in letters of fire on the darkness, and, sleepless, he would toss wearily to their refrain: "What doth it profit a man if he gain the whole world and suffer the loss of his own soul?" In the daytime, at the most brilliant point in his lecture, they would obtrude their unwelcome presence: "What doth it profit a man if he gain the whole world and suffer the loss of his own soul?"

The fight was long, but the day came when the young professor sought out Ignatius and asked him desperately what he was to do. In humble prayer and dependence he learned what was God's will for him. He might have been rector of the University of Beauvais—he was to be the greatest missioner the world has ever known.

So the first members of the Company of Jesus began to gather round their chief. Diego Lainez and Alfonso Salmeron, two young students of Alcalá, hearing of the fame of their countryman, came to Paris to seek him out and enlist under his standard. Nicholas Bobadilla, poor but of noble birth like Ignatius himself, threw in his lot with Loyola, as did Simon Rodriguez, gentle, handsome and amiable, but as yet without the active resourcefulness that he was later to develop.

In July 1534 the little band, seven in number, were invited to a meeting with their chief. After they had prayed together, Ignatius spoke.

His intention, he said, was to consecrate himself to God by vows of poverty, chastity and service in Palestine. He invited those who were of one mind with him to do likewise. Failing the chance of apostolic work in the Holy Land, they would go at a given time to Rome and place themselves at the Pope's service. Meanwhile, they were to pass the time in prayer, frequent reception of the Sacraments and study of the two books that were to remain always dearest to the heart of Ignatius, the Bible and the *Imitation of Christ*.

By these vows the seven companions bound themselves before the altar in the crypt of the chapel of St. Denis at Montmartre on the Feast of the Assumption, 1534, the Mass being said by Peter Favre, the only priest among them. Such was the foundation of the Company of Jesus.

But a fresh trial awaited the little band. This time it was not their preaching that excited suspicion, but their mysterious retirement. They were said to use a book—could it be an exposition of some of the new doctrines condemned by the Church? Ignatius was preparing to leave Paris, but he postponed his departure and prayed for a speedy inquiry. Laurent, the Inquisitor, requested that the "Exercises" should be shown to him; and, after reading the little work, was so delighted with it that he begged a copy for himself. Ignatius, having asked and obtained a formal attestation of his innocence, left Paris for Spain.

St. Ignatius and St. Francis Xavier at the
University of Paris

44

The First Vows at Montmartre

Chapter 7

THE WARFARE

IN the winter of 1536, Ignatius summoned his little band of disciples, who had remained behind in Paris to complete their studies, to meet him at Venice. He himself had spent the interval preaching in Spain and Italy, revisiting the scenes of his boyhood and founding in his native town of Azpeitia an association for the poor, which he endowed with the income from his own property. Don Martin, his brother, had strongly disapproved of the preaching and had prophesied with true brotherly candor that no one would listen. He soon learned his mistake, for Ignatius was fairly driven out of the town by the crowds which followed him; and in the country, when there was no more standing room around the preacher, the peasants climbed the trees.

The Spanish mission ended, Ignatius, on foot as usual, made his way to Venice to await the arrival of the travelers. Many had been their trials by the way. Sickness and peril, cold and want had been their portion; but, true soldiers of Christ, they had trudged on manfully to their journey's end, and in the meeting with their chief, all their woes were forgotten. For some time the little army, strengthened by recruits from Venice, worked together in the hospitals, young Francis Xavier sucking the wounds of the patients, a remedy then much believed in.

The time was now come to think of the projected mission to Palestine, but the league against the Turks made the seas impassable for pilgrims. To Loyola and his companions it was the hand of God that barred the way; they resolved to remain where they were. In the early summer of 1537, Ignatius and six others received ordination, and separating, the little army went forth two by two, as the Apostles of old, to preach the Gospel of Christ.

"Set all in fire and flame" were Ignatius' customary words of farewell to his companions, and with this precept in their hearts they spoke.

Everywhere at their burning words faith and love rekindled; clergy and people cast off the bonds that held them and awoke to a new life. But the success was never to be uninterrupted for long. The old accusation of heresy was brought up, to be once more publicly and triumphantly refuted. Then it was that Ignatius resolved to undertake the long postponed journey to Rome.

Setting out in company with Favre and Lainez, he arrived at the Eternal City in the late autumn. On the way thither, while he was praying in a wayside chapel, Our Lord appeared to him in a vision, bending under the burden of the Cross.

"I will have you to serve Me," He said; "I will be propitious to you in Rome."

To Paul III, engaged as he was in the laborious and difficult work of reform, the proffered service of Ignatius was very welcome. Favre and Lainez he appointed at once to lecture at the University, while Ignatius devoted himself to his beloved poor. In the spring of 1538, the disciples, whose mission had been abundantly blessed by God, were recalled to Rome, where they found Ignatius established in a house that had been given to the Society by its first Roman member. Rome for the time was to be their field of action, and there the apostolate began in good earnest. As in Venice, before their burning zeal the fire kindled and men changed their lives.

As in Venice also, the enemy of mankind was active against them. The Pope had left the city to confer with Francis I and Charles V on the subject of a proposed Crusade. The moment was ripe.

Francis Xavier, when a student in Paris, had had a young friend, one Miguel Navarro, whose anger and jealousy had been aroused by his conversion. Climbing up one night to the window of Ignatius' room with a dagger between his teeth, Navarro had determined to put an end once for all to his influence over the young professor; but a voice from Heaven struck terror to his guilty soul. Falling at the feet of his intended victim, he confessed his sin and implored pardon. The conversion seemed genuine; he even joined the Society, but soon left it—to seek readmission at a later period. This was, however, refused him, and, resolved on vengeance, he joined forces with one Fra Agostino, an Augustinian friar and secret disciple of Luther. They came to Rome, where the friar began at once to preach, drawing large audiences.

At first all seemed to be well, but gradually the Lutheran doctrines insinuated themselves, and the watchful began to see how the wind was blowing. Lainez and Salmeron privately warned Agostino that his teaching was unorthodox, but an insulting defiance was the only reply. The friar then resolved on a bold move. From the pulpit he openly denounced Ignatius and his disciples as heretics. Three times, he declared, had they been tried and convicted: in Salamanca, Paris and Venice. He had witnesses to prove the truth of all he said. Navarro was produced, and the tide of popular feeling began to turn against the Jesuits. Ignatius was advised to appeal to

Cardinal de Cupis, the head of the Sacred College, but the Cardinal was strongly against him and refused him audience. A mutual friend at last prevailed on him to change his mind, but it was sorely against the grain.

"Let him come," the Cardinal said, "but he shall get what he deserves."

Ignatius came, and the two were alone for a time together. Once again, as so many times before, contact with the man converted the bitterest enemy into the warmest friend. The Cardinal himself accompanied his visitor to the door, proffering all the help in his power. Ignatius requested an instant trial, that he might be confronted by his enemies.

Navarro repeated his charge, but on Loyola's producing a letter written by Miguel himself, warm in praise of the little Company and of their chief, the evidence broke down completely. Agostino professed himself ready to recant, but Ignatius was resolved to put an end once for all to these continued assaults which promised to be such a hindrance to the work of the Society. On the Pope's return he laid the whole matter before him, and the proceedings were again opened.

By the extraordinary Providence of God, the three very men who had tried and acquitted Ignatius at Alcalá, Paris and Venice were all together in Rome at the time, and they united their evidence in his favor. Testimonies came from all districts where Ignatius' disciples had worked, and their innocence was formally attested. Navarro and Agostino were forced to flee from Rome to escape the punishment of their calumny.

At Christmas of 1538 Ignatius said his very first Mass, and then he turned his attention to a work of mercy that was sadly in need of volunteers. Famine was in Rome, and the people were dying of hunger in the streets. Over four hundred were sheltered in the new house of the Company, tended, fed and clothed. The rich, moved by their example, gave generously. The Pope was learning the value of the little army of devoted men who feared neither hardship nor labor in the service of Christ.

It was in these early days at Rome that Pedro Ribadeneira joined the Company of Jesus.

This madcap boy of fifteen was a page in the household of Cardinal Farnese, kinsman of Paul III, and many were the pranks he played. At a stately function where the Pope himself was present, and the pages of the household were in attendance with lighted torches, he had dashed from the ranks to beat a brother page about the head because, as he remarked indignantly, he had made a face at him.

The Cardinal having one day ordered his attendance on a short journey into the country, Pedro, whose fancy the country did not please, ran off and spent the day strolling about the town. With nightfall came the prospect of a thrashing from the master of the pages; so, remembering opportunely that he had promised a friend to visit Ignatius when in Rome, the runaway knocked at the door of the Jesuit house and found himself face to face with Loyola on the doorstep. The two understood each other at once, and on the boy's explaining the situation to his new friend, Ignatius offered him a bed and promised to intercede for him on the morrow.

The Cardinal only laughed, for Pedro was a general favorite, and told them to send him back; but a fresh complication had arisen. Back Pedro would not go. He liked Ignatius; he liked the Fathers; they suited him; he was going to remain; he would be a Jesuit too. No persuasions could prevail on him to change his mind, and in the end, with the consent of his family, Ignatius kept him. Then began such a noviceship as surely no religious house had seen before.

It was not in a day, nor yet in a year, that the reckless, willful nature of Ribadeneira was to learn the "strength that comes of self-control." The pranks he played were endless; the noise he made was unparalleled. The novice master complained again and again that the boy would never do any good. Ignatius alone saw all the possibilities that lay hidden under the wild, untamed nature. Such a character would be strong for good or evil; here was no nonentity, but Ignatius did not like nonentities.

"If Pedro lives," he would say, "he will do great things for God."

Ribadeneira's love and admiration for his master were boundless, and he tried his best to please him, though his efforts were not always crowned with success.

By degrees, with a persevering patience, Ignatius led him to make the Exercises. After that, things went better, though two years later, when the boy was sent to the University of Paris, we catch a glimpse of the old mischievous spirit still alive. The little party lodged for a night in the hospital at Viterbo. Here Pedro amused himself by a voyage of discovery which ended in the church. Climbing into the pulpit he made as if he were addressing an imaginary congregation, while the old sexton, who had been sweeping in a corner, promptly set to work to ring the bell. It was the hour for a sermon; the people flocked in.

"But who is going to preach?" asked Pedro, a little taken aback.

"You, of course," replied the sacristan.

Here was a situation!

The novice was luckily not troubled by shyness; a few weeks before, he had been obliged, as were all novices in the Society, to preach a trial sermon before the community. Happily he remembered it, and he gave it out in his best manner; although, the ordeal once over, he was not sorry to make his escape. But not so fast! He was waylaid by an old man who had kept a grudge against a neighbor for years. The sermon, he said, had done him good; he wanted to go to Confession. Pedro fetched one of his companions who was a priest, and he congratulated himself that his prank had had no worse ending.

Ignatius' prophecy was fulfilled; the madcap Pedro became in later years a true and faithful soldier of Christ and one of the most famous writers of the Society.

Chapter 8

THE GENERAL AND HIS ARMY

THE little Company of Jesus had now taken its stand amongst the "regulars" of the Church. It was a religious order, lately approved by the Pope, of which Ignatius had been elected General for life by every vote in the Society but his own. Failing utterly to convince his companions by the protest that any man of them all would have made a better General than himself, he proceeded to inaugurate the new honor by working for a week in the kitchen. It was now time to look abroad and see what was to be done for God.

Up to the present time the religious orders had concerned themselves chiefly with missions to the people. These were not to be neglected, but Ignatius could not fail to see that as yet little had been done for those of a higher rank. His apostolate at the universities had been fruitful; here the Society, whose members were drawn largely, like Ignatius himself, from the upper classes, was destined to influence strongly the intellectual life of the world. The "humanists" of the Renaissance, who held that piety and learning could hardly exist together, were to find men as learned and cultured as themselves, strong and steadfast in the Faith. The Reformers, who urged the worldliness of the clergy as a reason for forsaking the Creed of their fathers, were to find priests and religious teachers whose holiness and simplicity of life put their own utterly to shame. Two by two, the little army went forth once more, this time to the centers of unbelief. Siena, Parma, Worms, Regensburg, Innsbruck, Vienna, in turn felt their influence. Colleges were founded everywhere for the secular as well as the religious training of boys and young men, for no one knew better than Ignatius the importance of an education that should be both wise and thorough for the rising generation.

The year 1541 saw the birth of the first great missionary enterprise of the Society to the heathen. The King of Portugal, John III, who had great possessions in the Indies, was seeking for men to preach Christianity to the natives of India. The new Society was recommended to him as likely to furnish what he required, and Ignatius' long-desired opportunity of preaching to the heathen was at last within his grasp. Gladly would he have led the little band himself, but his ill health and advancing years prevented this.

Bobadilla and Rodriguez were offered for the work, but Bobadilla was down with rheumatism and unfit for the journey. Ignatius turned to Francis Xavier, who had been working at Bologna with the combined zeal and sweetness that made his apostolate as fruitful at home as it was to be later in heathen lands.

"God wills to use you for this mission," Ignatius said.

"Father, I am ready," was the reply.

The outfit of the future Apostle of the Indies consisted of an old worn-out cassock, carefully mended by his own hands, and a breviary.

Ignatius, who was ill at the time and wearing a warmer garment than usual, took it off and wrapped it around him. The next day the little party started out.

On the voyage, the Admiral would have had the Jesuits to dine with him at his own table, but this they would not do, so he was forced to content himself with sending them part of what was served for his own use. This Francis distributed among the sick poor on board, whom he had gathered in his own cabin to tend and care for. The fragments left by the passengers were thought by the missioners to be good enough for them.

Of Francis' labors in India, this is not the place to tell; he died as he had lived, amid hardships and dangers, having won thousands to the knowledge and love of Christ.

Ignatius had now passed his fiftieth year. The austerities of earlier days had told so severely on his health that, grown wiser by experience, he watched carefully lest his younger companions should go beyond their strength in these matters. The sackcloth gown of Manresa had also been discarded long ago as unsuitable to the work of the Society. The Jesuits were to go about neat and clean, though poverty was to be strictly observed. Ignatius was of one mind with his great compatriot, St. Teresa, in his hatred of slovenliness and dirt. Yet he would mend the rents in his garments carefully and lovingly, saying of them, "These are the livery of my Lord."

Equally great was his hatred of anything that savored of untruthfulness or of deceit; he considered such things, he used to say, unworthy of a well-born and educated man, still less of a Christian.

He strove to impress on his sons the nobility of any kind of work that was done for God, from the labors of the brother in the kitchen to those of the preacher in the church.

"For whom are you working?" he asked one day of a lay brother who was sweeping in a very half-hearted manner.

"For God," was the answer.

"Then you deserve a good penance," replied the General sternly. "If you were working for men, it would not so much matter, but work for God should be better done than that."

The life of Jesus was to be their example, said the Jesuit rule; the sinner should be dear to every one in the Society. Never were they to neglect an opportunity of doing good, but if it should please God to work great things through their means, they were to count themselves as nothing. Prayer and humility were to be the backbone of their spiritual life, and studies were to be deep and thorough.

The General moreover demanded a very perfect obedience from his men. His experience as a soldier had taught him that herein lies all the strength of an army.

> Theirs not to reason why,
> Theirs but to do or die

is true heroism, and Ignatius knew it. There is profound wisdom in the truth that "he who ruleth his spirit is better than he that taketh a city." One of the chief characteristics of the Society was to be its perfect discipline; its organization was to be that of an army. At sixty years of age, Ignatius declared that the slightest sign from the Pope would send him aboard the first ship in the harbor, bound for any port in the world.

"That would not be very prudent," observed a nobleman who was present.

"Prudence, my lord," said the hero of Pamplona, "is the virtue for those who command, not for those who obey."

Ignatius required from his men a devotion that considered nothing impossible that was bidden them. All great generals have required the same, and it has been one of the secrets of their success.

For men of a mutinous and discontented spirit the Saint had no use. Such was not the stuff of which the soldiers of Christ were to be made. Grumbling at orders given was a bad note. It was once reported to him that a novice, who was displeased at something he had been told to do, was going about saying that he would leave the Society the very next day.

"That he shall not," said Ignatius, "he shall go tonight." And go that night he did.

On the other hand, he was full of sympathy for the difficulties of fiery, hot-tempered natures. He liked them, and he believed, as in the case of Ribadeneira, that self-mastery once obtained, they would often go farther and do better work for God than their gentler brethren. "Conquer thyself," he would often repeat to such firebrands, encouraging and helping them in moments of difficulty; and many there were who owed their perseverance to his understanding sympathy.

Another great characteristic of Ignatius was his tender care for the sick. He used to say that he believed that God had sent him so much sickness that he might help and sympathize with others. If any were ill in the house, he would visit them frequently, watching by them if necessary at night, making their beds and tending them in all things with a father's care. He wrote kind letters to those of his sons who were ill in other lands. If any delicacy was ordered for an invalid, Ignatius insisted that he should have it, even though the community should have to dine on bread in consequence, or beg their food in the streets.

To endure affliction for Christ's sake, he would say, was the highest gain, and to love God with all one's heart, one's soul and one's will, the greatest good. He had a great love for plants and flowers, and all that beauty of the outside world so suggestive to pure and thoughtful minds of the beauty which is eternal. To him indeed earth was

> crammed with heaven,
> And every common bush afire with God.

A friend who knew Ignatius well described

him thus:

"His very appearance seemed to make everyone who saw him better, and so reproved all meanness and wickedness that no one with a bad conscience could have looked him in the face."

On his first arrival in Rome, Ignatius had made a vow to accept for himself and his companions neither honors nor dignity; but the success of his sons in their apostolic work bade fair to be an obstacle to the determination. Over and over again one or other of the Society would be proposed by princes or rulers for a bishopric; more especially was this the case in Germany. The vow was to accept no honors save at the direct command of the Pope, and now crowned heads were appealing to the Vicar of Christ to compel the reluctant Fathers to submit. Ignatius was alarmed, and himself appealed to the Pope.

"It would be a danger to the very spirit of the Company. The other orders in the Church," argued the old soldier, "were like squadrons of cuirassiers, whose duty was to stand fast in their appointed places and face the enemy. For them such honors were meet. But the Company of Jesus was a body of light horsemen always ready to go in any direction in skirmishing order at the sign of the Vicar of Christ. It was not in their nature to be fixed in one place."

"This is the first time that I have heard such a petition," said the Pope, but he gave way. The danger, however, was to arise again later.

The reader remembers the meeting of Ignatius, on his way to prison in Alcalá, with young Francis Borgia, son of the Duke of Gandia. The world had prospered with Borgia since the meeting; he had won fame for himself on the field of battle, married the wife of his heart and was the trusted friend and confidant of the Emperor Charles V. On the death of the Empress Isabella he was chosen to accompany the funeral procession to Granada and to identify the body when there.

The coffin was opened, and Francis was confronted with the remains of the beautiful woman whom he had known so well. Death had made terrible havoc with those fair features, and the sight made such a profound impression on Borgia of the emptiness of the things of this world that he resolved, as soon as it should be possible, to enter religion. Not long after, his beloved wife died, and Francis Borgia was admitted to the Society of Jesus.

The event made a great stir in Spain, and the Emperor wrote to the Pope, requesting that his friend might be made a Cardinal.

Borgia fled from Rome to avoid the unwelcome dignity, and Ignatius again appealed to Christ's

Vicar for protection. It was agreed that to please the Emperor the Cardinal's hat should be offered, but on the refusal of Francis, the matter should be dropped, and Ignatius breathed again.

The mission of this new son of the Society was to be to Spain. There his great influence did much for the Jesuits. Colleges and churches were built, and the work of evangelization made great progress.

After the death of Lainez, who succeeded St. Ignatius, St. Francis Borgia would be made General of the Society of Jesus, which he would govern with a holiness and wisdom second only to that of the great founder himself.

St. Ignatius and St. Francis Borgia before the
Altar of Santa Maria della Strada

St. Ignatius and companions in the presence of Pope
Paul III, who approved the Society of Jesus in 1540.

Chapter 9

"AD MAJOREM DEI GLORIAM"

WE have seen how, already in the days of Ignatius' university life at Alcalá and Paris, men could find no other explanation of his extraordinary influence over others than that of sorcery. In the sixteenth century, witchcraft and enchantment were believed by many, even educated men, to be very widespread, and anything extraordinary was satisfactorily put down to their practice. But the belief in sorcery was to die down, and the influence of the Jesuits was to remain. The cunning and the wiliness of the sons of St. Ignatius, said their enemies, explained it all. The fact that wiliness and cunning did not produce quite the same effect when employed by other people, they did not consider worth their notice.

The "wiles" of the Society of Jesus had indeed a deeper root than the world suspected, and they had learned them from a teacher greater than Ignatius himself. When the Master whose name it was their honor to bear made His dwelling

among men, it was said of Him in contempt
that He ate and drank with publicans and sinners. The name "Friend of sinners" must have
indeed been dear to the heart of Christ, but it
was nonetheless used by His enemies as a term
of reproach. St. Paul, the great Apostle of the
Gentiles, was only treading in his Lord's footsteps when he said, "I became all things to all
men that I might save all." Herein lies the secret
of that power of the Society of Jesus which has
been so much and so often misunderstood and
misrepresented. A holiness that draws back its
skirts from the erring multitude may be respected
and feared; it will be neither loved nor followed.

Ignatius was never tired of impressing on his
sons in Christ the necessity of a large-minded
and understanding charity in dealing with men,
for whom, though they might be living in error
or in sin, as much excuse was to be found as
they in like case would find for themselves.

"There, but for the grace of God, goes Charles
Wesley," said the famous Protestant preacher on
seeing a criminal going to execution. The feeling is that of all honest men who know themselves.

"I go in at their door, but I am careful to
make them come out at mine," said St. Francis
Xavier, or in other words, "I interest myself in
what interests them, that I may lead them to

interest themselves in the things of God." It was
a "wile" that he had learned of his Master, Christ,
no less than of his spiritual father, Ignatius.

The reader may remember Ortiz, the erstwhile
enemy of Loyola, who later became one of his
most faithful friends. He determined when at
Rome to make the Exercises under the Saint's
direction, and for a time all went well. But Ortiz
was not used to solitary prayer, and the loneliness told on his spirits. He gave way to depres-
sion and had almost resolved to give it all up,
when Ignatius entered and, seeing at a glance
how things were going, asked him if he remembered the national dance. Ortiz, like Ignatius
himself, was a Spaniard, and he resembled all
his countrymen in his love of dancing; he cheered
up a little at the question and forgot to be low-
spirited.

Then the Saint, calling up all the skill of his
youthful days, danced for the greater glory of
God, to the delight and enthusiasm of his
retreatant. Ortiz took heart and resolved to go
on with the Exercises. He persevered to the end
and came out having learned, he said, more theology in four weeks than he had taught, doctor
though he was, in his whole life.

When Ignatius was in Paris, he went one day
to visit a French doctor of theology, better known
as a gambler than as a theologian. The French-

man, half in jest, invited his guest to a game of billiards, which invitation, perhaps a little to his surprise, the visitor accepted.

"But," said Ignatius, "you are accustomed to play for money, and I have none; I will therefore make a proposal. If you win, I will be your servant for a month; if I beat you, you will be at my disposition for the same time, and I promise that it will be for your advantage."

The idea took the gambler's fancy; the risk besides would not be great. Ignatius could not be much of a player; the Frenchman thought himself safe.

But he had reckoned without his host; the Spaniard won and promptly demanded his stake. The doctor was to make the Spiritual Exercises then and there under Ignatius' direction. There was no help for it; the unwilling retreatant began the Exercises. The prayers of the Saint and of the sinner together did their work, and in this strange way another soul was won from a life of sin to the service of God.

In this way would Ignatius interest himself in all things that concerned those with whom he came in contact. He would talk of war with the soldier, of commerce with the merchant, of their work with the poor; yet all who spoke to him felt themselves the better for the meeting.

In the early days at Venice, Ignatius and his

companions had baptized and sheltered in their house a young Jew who desired to become a Christian. His elder brother, hearing of the conversion, pursued the boy to Venice and tracked him to his hiding place. In a state of great indignation he confronted the Fathers, who received him with gentle charity and an invitation to remain under their roof that he might be better able to converse with his brother.

In the evening, according to the custom of the house, they washed his feet, and so touched his heart by their kindness that he also in due time embraced the Faith. He afterward became a missionary in the East, where his knowledge of the Oriental tongues made him a valuable worker.

Later, when the Society was established in Rome, a young Lutheran, noted for his eloquence, came to preach in the city and was arrested and imprisoned for denying the doctrines of the Church. Ignatius interceded for the delinquent and asked that he should be allowed to come to them that they might see what they could do on his behalf. The request was granted, and the unwilling guest, very much on the defensive and determined not to be moved by anything his hosts should say, awaited the moment of attack. But the attack did not come; he was treated by everyone in the house with the greatest consideration and charity, and all questions of doctrine were carefully avoided. A month or two later, he was reconciled to the Church.

"We knew that you would be converted by their arguments," said his friends contemptuously, when he left Rome.

"Their arguments did not convert me," replied the young man, "it was the lives they led. 'Men who live like this,' I said to myself, 'must have the truth with them.'"

The first rector of the house at Alcalá was Francisco de Villanueva, who like Favre was the son of poor and ignorant peasants. Ignatius used to say of the humble and intelligent novice that he had courage enough for anything and that he would be glad to have twenty more like him in the Society.

At Alcalá, in spite of the fact that his wisdom and holiness brought men of the highest rank to seek his advice and guidance, his favorite employment was to help in the kitchen, which he would declare was the right place for such as he. Villanueva had a friend, one Pedro de Aragon, a monk at the convent of Tendilla, a few miles from Alcalá, who, yielding to the persuasion of the Jesuit, made the Exercises under his direction. The profit he derived was so great that, on his return to the monastery, he advised all the brethren to follow his example; but the proposal was treated with contempt.

They had grown old in religion, they replied, and had nothing to learn from a young religious and a new order. One only, and that one more from a spirit of contradiction than from anything else, resolved to take the step, his resolution being received with a good deal of merriment. This was an old soldier of such a peppery disposition and uncertain temper that he was only retained in the house on account of the large sums of money he had bestowed on it.

This rather unpromising candidate set off for Alcalá in not the most humble of dispositions and requested to see the rector. But when he was confronted by Villanueva, diffident in manner and wearing a patched old cassock, his disgust knew no bounds, and he was for returning home on the spot. A soft answer, however, turneth away wrath, and somewhat pacified by the gracious charity with which his not over-polite remarks were met, he agreed to stay the night and next day consented to begin his retreat.

In his case the four weeks of the Exercises had to be considerably lengthened, but the old nobleman persevered, and when he at length returned to his monastery, the haughty and violent-tempered monk had become gentle and humble. His brethren, in deep astonishment, waited to see how long the transformation was going to last; but though the struggle was sometimes apparent, the change was thorough and enduring. They one and all resolved to take the means to effect a like change in themselves, and made the Exercises with great benefit.

It was this desire to do all for the greater glory of God and to be all things to all men that made the Jesuit missioners to China and Japan adopt the customs and even the dress of the natives. Living thus in the center of their flock, making its interests their own, they would lead men almost imperceptibly to God and so change the face of the land. It was the working out of their great founder's lifelong maxim: *Ad Majorem Dei Gloriam*—"For the greater glory of God."

Chapter 10

THE LAST FIGHT

IN the year 1548, the long-postponed Council of Trent, so ardently desired by all loyal lovers of the Church, held its first assembly. Its object was the definition of those doctrines which had been assailed by the sects of Luther and Calvin and the renovation of the inner life of the Church by the reform of certain abuses that had crept in unawares during the years of relaxation. The Council was held in the cathedral of Trent, with two future Popes, Cardinals del Monte and Cervini, assisted by a famous Englishman, Cardinal Pole, presiding as papal legates.

All Christian princes were begged to send prelates from their different dominions to the Council, and no less than thirty-six ambassadors, eleven Archbishops, sixty-nine Bishops, seven Generals of religious orders and over eighty theologians and doctors were present. It was hardly to be expected that the members of the Company of Jesus, who held neither rank nor dignity in the Church, would form part of such an illustrious assembly. Yet in Germany, Belgium and Austria, the sons of St. Ignatius were chosen by princes and prelates as their theologians. The Pope himself named Salmeron and Lainez as Papal theologians, perhaps a little to the dismay of Ignatius; for Salmeron was but thirty years of age and absurdly boyish in appearance, while Lainez was only some four years older. It was true that both were carefully trained, learned and eloquent; still, the responsibility was great.

The General of the Jesuits laid down careful rules for their conduct. They were to set forth the arguments on both sides of a question, to avoid sharp or wounding words and to speak with calmness, peace and modesty. In all they did in the Council, as well as outside of it, their sole motive was to be the glory of God and the good of the Church. Nor were they, on account of their onerous duties, to consider themselves free from the Jesuit rule of visiting the hospitals, preaching to the poor and teaching the catechism to children. With these injunctions he blessed them both and bade them go in the name of Christ. It was the influence of Ignatius himself that was to emanate from his sons, and his spirit that was to speak in them.

The assembly in the cathedral was magnificent indeed and worthy of the brush of the great painter Titian. The scarlet robes of the Cardinals, the golden mitres and the purple of the bishops, the white, brown and gray of the friars' habits mingled with the black of the Benedictine monks and of the secular clergy in a rich harmony of color. The vaulted roof and the fluted columns of the cathedral made a background at once somber and rich.

Among all this splendor the patched cassocks of the Pope's theologians excited some comment. Several of the clergy went so far as to say that it was scarcely respectful to appear at such a great assembly so shabbily clad. Lainez and Salmeron therefore accepted the new cassocks provided for them by their countrymen, but were careful to wear them only when at the sessions of the Council.

It was not long before those present were to see the wisdom of the Pope's choice. The discourses of Salmeron won general admiration; but when Lainez rose to speak, the wonder and enthusiasm were unbounded, for his learning was only equalled by his extraordinary memory. In his discourse on the Blessed Eucharist he quoted by heart thirty-six Doctors of the Church, in all of whose writings he was thoroughly at home, and on being asked with some surprise if he had read all the works of one of these authors, voluminous as they were, he answered: "I have read them, re-read them, and read them again." On account of his convincing and unanswerable arguments, the best theologians accepted his decision as final.

The orators present were seldom as a rule permitted to speak for an hour at a time, but Lainez was allowed three, and no one tired of listening to him. His task it was to recapitulate the discussions at the end of the day, and as his voice was weak, a special place was reserved for him in the midst of the bishops. The Council was to be interrupted several times, but Lainez to the end remained one of its brightest lights, and the remark of an ecclesiastic present that he was glad to live in an age when he might listen to such men, who were as learned as they were good, expressed the sentiments of many others.

In the year 1555 the German College was founded in Rome and throve prosperously, as did its companion, the Roman College, under the administration of the Jesuits. One of the dreams of Ignatius' heart had been the more careful training of young men destined for the priesthood, and it was now fulfilled.

The foundation of these two colleges was his greatest work. The Roman College had been begun with donations from several people, among them Francis Borgia, the Duke of Gandia. The Pope bestowed on it the privilege of a university, and in 1555 it numbered two hundred pupils who had come from all parts of the world. The professors were Jesuits, chosen from among the most learned men of the Society. The classes were attended by students from fourteen colleges in Rome, as well as by those of the Jesuits themselves who were going through their training.

Ignatius took the greatest interest in their progress and arranged that public disputations should take place from time to time among the students, to which he would invite Cardinals and distinguished theologians. Among its students have been seven Popes and many Saints.

The German College was founded to raise the tone of the German clergy, who were often ignorant and wanting in zeal for souls. Our old friend Ribadeneira was among its first professors.

The year 1552 saw the death of Francis Xavier, the most saintly and gifted of Ignatius' sons. After a long and successful apostolate in India, he had resolved to preach the Faith to the natives of China. Embarking at Malacca, he landed on the island of Sancian, a desolate rock lying off the Chinese coast. On his arrival he was attacked by a violent fever and was soon at the point of death. Alone and deserted, abandoned by the crew of the ship in which he had sailed, the man who had gained nations and kingdoms to Christ lay exposed to the scorching sun of the

day and the piercing blasts of the night, home-
less and a wanderer on the earth.

A Chinese convert in company with a Por-
tuguese merchant who had just landed on the
island discovered the Saint lying on the ground
with his crucifix clasped to his breast, murmuring
even in the delirium of fever the words that
through life had been most often on his lips,
"My God and my All." They bore him to a little hut and watched by his side until with words
of love and confidence he lifted his radiant face
to Heaven and passed into the presence of the
Lord whom he had served so faithfully.

For many years after, the vessels that passed
the island of Sancian would lower their flags and
salute the spot where the Apostle of India had
breathed his last.

Ignatius was now over sixty years of age, and
so weak in body that he knew that his days were
numbered. The prospect of a speedy death filled
him with joy. The light of the other world already
shone in his eyes; his was, as his sons used to
say, "a face for Paradise." So worn was he with
fasting and penance, joined to continual ill-
health, that it seemed a wonder that he had
lived so long. Nevertheless, he would spare himself in nothing, going through his daily duties
in spite of weakness and fatigue. His room was
poor, and the little furniture that was in it was

of the meanest description. His whole library consisted of the Bible, the Breviary, and the *Imitation of Christ*.

His heart was with God even when he was at work, and he would constantly raise his eyes to Heaven, as if to seek rest for a moment in the presence of his Lord. That bright face, "radiant with divine beauty," as said the Cardinal Archbishop of Toledo, made a deep impression of sanctity on all who saw it. It was at this time that he remarked to a friend that the three desires of his heart had been granted. His order was officially recognized by the Pope; the book of the *Spiritual Exercises* was approved; and the Constitutions completed and observed by the Society all the world over. Those who heard him guessed at his meaning. It was time for him to say his *Nunc Dimittis*; his life was nearing its end. Yet his interest and his zeal for souls never slackened.

A short time before his death, Ignatius heard that when, during the carnival of Macerata, a play was to be acted that might do harm to young people, the Fathers of the Society had ordered exposition of the Blessed Sacrament for three days, with the result that the people had flocked to the church and given up the play. Ignatius was so pleased with this idea that he ordered that the devotion of the *Quarant' Ore*

("Forty Hours") should take place in all the houses of the Society during the carnival. The practice has since extended to the whole Church.

Ignatius' health was rapidly failing. During the hot summer days of 1556, he retired to the country house of the Society outside the walls of Rome, but he soon returned to the city that he might be with his beloved sons. Several Fathers in the house were ill, among them Lainez. Ignatius had a slight fever, but he had been ailing so long that no immediate danger was feared; indeed, some of the patients seemed worse than he.

One afternoon he sent for Father Polanco and asked him to go to St. Peter's to tell the Pope that he was near his end and to beg his prayers and blessing. Polanco replied that the doctor had insisted that Ignatius was in no danger, and that they hoped God would preserve him to the Society for many years to come.

"Do you feel so ill?" he said.

"So ill," replied the Saint, "that nothing remains for me but to give up my soul to God."

Still Polanco maintained that he was mistaken. Might he wait for a day or two, he asked, before taking the message, as he had important letters to write for Spain and desired to catch the post? Ignatius answered wistfully that he had rather it be done at once, but Polanco was to do what he thought best. Once more the latter besought the doctor to tell him if Ignatius was in danger of death.

"I cannot pronounce today," was the answer; "I will tell you tomorrow."

Polanco resolved to wait. That evening the Saint seemed better: he took supper as usual and talked brightly to those who were with him. The infirmarian who watched by him at night reported that he had been restless till midnight, but then became quiet, only murmuring from time to time a short prayer.

At daybreak the doctors arrived. They found him weak but had no idea that the end was near. "Give him some strengthening food," they ordered, but while the infirmarian was preparing it, one of the Fathers, who had just entered, saw that the Saint was at the point of death. He went to call the others, but before he returned, Ignatius was no more. He passed away in peace and calmness with the Holy Name on his lips.

His sons wept for their father with aching hearts, but they firmly believed that he would continue to guide and intercede for his Society in Heaven. Lainez, who was still ill and unable to rise from his bed, read the sad truth in the faces of those around him. He implored of God to take him too, and besought the Saint to obtain this grace by his prayers. But such was not God's will. Lainez recovered, to be elected General in his beloved father's place.

Still in death lay that great heart that had given up all dreams of earthly glory for love of the Crucified, to embrace a life of poverty and suffering.

The great intellect that had organized an army that was to fight the battles of Christ in every country of the world was face to face with the Wisdom which is Eternal.

He had fought the good fight and conquered. Henceforward there was laid up for him a crown of glory.

Ignatius was beatified by Pope Paul V in the year 1609, and in 1622 he was raised to the altars of the Church by Pope Gregory XV. The prosperity of his order, for it *has* prospered in spite of persecution and calumny, is due to the fact that the qualities of its holy founder have been its life and soul. The army of St. Ignatius has outlasted the armies of Spain and has made greater conquests than those of Cortez or Pizarro.

Chapter 11

THE LEGACY

IT was often remarked during the lifetime of St. Ignatius, that if the Society enjoyed for any length of time (and this was rare) untroubled peace and prosperity, the General would become anxious and uneasy. He was a firm believer in the truth that "Whom the Lord loveth, He chastiseth, and scourgeth every son whom He receiveth." The Cross for him was the very seal of God's approval on his work; without it, he feared that all might not be well.

We are told that Ignatius, coming out of his oratory one day with a joyously radiant face, was met by Ribadeneira, who asked him, "What grace has God given to you, Father, that you look so happy?"

"Our Lord," replied the Saint, "has promised me, in answer to my earnest prayer, that the Society shall never be without the Cross."

Never has a promise been more faithfully fulfilled. "You shall be hated by all men for My Name's sake" became true indeed of the Com-

von Matt

Portrait of St. Ignatius painted on the day of his death by
Jacopino del Conte, one of the Saint's former penitents.

Portrait of St. Ignatius by Sánches Coello, Philip II's court painter, commissioned by Ribadeneira after the Saint's death. St. Ignatius refused to have his portrait painted during his life.

pany of Jesus from the moment it bore the name of Jesus. The very title "Jesuit" was a term of contempt, originally bestowed on the sons of Ignatius by Calvin, who had his reasons for disliking them.

The spirit in which the Saint was wont to meet expressions of open enmity is delightfully shown by a letter addressed to a gentleman who had conveyed to him an abusive missive from a Spanish friar:

"Sir,

"Pray tell Fray Barbarán that as he declares that he would wish that all of ours who are living between Perpignan and Seville may be burnt [as heretics], I declare and I wish that all his friends and acquaintances, not only between Perpignan and Seville, but all whom the world contains, may be fired and inflamed by the Holy Ghost, so that they may all come to great perfection and be very distinguished in the glory of His Divine Majesty.

"So, too, you will tell him that our affairs are being gone into before the Governor [of Rome] and the Vicar of His Holiness, and a sentence is soon to be pronounced. If he have anything against us, I invite him to depose to it and to prove it before these judges. For I should prefer, if guilty, to pay for it, and to suffer for it, in

my own person, than that all those between Perpignan and Seville should be burnt.

"IÑIGO"

But it is easier to deal with an open foe than
a secret slanderer.

From the account of the Last Supper it is evi-
dent that the Apostles were entirely ignorant of
the treachery of Judas, even though he had been
living with them in the closest intimacy. Sin had
crept, at first almost imperceptibly, into his heart,
gradually taking possession of the whole man
until, in the terrible words of the Gospel, "Satan
entered into him." In the Society of Jesus, as in
all religious orders, there have been traitors too,
men who have gradually given way to the temptations of the evil one, until their real character
could lie no longer hidden and they stood revealed
in their true colors. Nothing remained for that
Company, with which they had no longer anything in common, but to cut off the rotten branch
from the tree and expel the unworthy member.

The world would hesitate to accept as trust-
worthy the testimony of a clerk dismissed for
misconduct against the business firm who had
dismissed him; the evidence of a servant sent
away without a reference would be taken with
caution against her mistress. Yet the witness of
one expelled from the Society has always been

accepted by many as unquestionably fair and truthful, no matter how monstrous his assertions may be.

He knows more about the matter and is altogether more to be trusted than the body which has expelled him. He has lived among the Jesuits and knows them; his expulsion is, of course, due to the fact that he is too honest and upright a man for such a community. So reason the enemies of the Society. Such men as these have been among the most bitter of its antagonists and have done the most to blacken its reputation.

Such was Zahorowski, the inventor of the "*Monita Secreta*" or "Secret Orders," a supposed code of instructions known only to the superiors of the Society, by which they are bound to enrich and exalt their order by any means in their power, be they fair or foul.

"If pitch is thrown," the saying goes, "some will stick"; and in spite of the fact that the story of the "*Monita Secreta*" was pronounced by the Cardinals of the Holy Congregation to be "false, defamatory and calumnious," there remain to this day people who believe it. This, however, was only the first of a series of slanders that were to continue even to our own days. Who has not heard the story that a Jesuit is compelled to obey his superior even though he should be ordered to commit a murder? Now a Jesuit's vow of obedience binds him to do what his superior commands "in as far as these commands entail nothing sinful, contrary to the law of God or the just laws of the State." But there are always people to be found who know more about the rules and customs of religious than they do themselves, and prejudices die hard.

That the Society gives its members permission, and even encourages them to "do evil that good may come" is another calumny that still finds many believers, though not among those familiar with the teaching of the Catholic Church— that if a man might save the whole world by committing one venial sin, it would be wrong to do it.

Ignatius himself would meet all such calumnies (always excepting accusations of heresy) with a determined silence and would tell his brethren that to live the slanders down was their best and wisest defense. To return good for evil, or if this were not possible, to ignore the evil, was his plan of action in all cases, and he lived to see its wisdom. The lives of the Jesuits, their labors, their humility, their poverty, their patience, are answer enough.

"Let all our study be to have an upright intention, not only in our state of life in general, but also in our particular actions, proposing nothing else to ourselves than to serve and please God, and this rather through love and gratitude to Him than through fear of punishment or hope of reward."

This is the end set before the Society by its holy founder in the Constitutions. How far that end has been attained is known to God. Of all races, of all nations, and in all climes, yet one in aim and effort, the sons of St. Ignatius for hundreds of years have labored on the earth with the teaching of their Father in their hearts. What has been the result?

The Society of Jesus counts on its roll thirteen canonized Saints [as of 1919], countless martyrs and many others who have been named "Blessed" or "Venerable" by the Church. Among these, not to mention the glorious names of St. Francis Xavier, Bl. Peter Favre, (or Faber) and St. Francis Borgia, with whom we are already familiar, are to be counted St. Peter Canisius, the brilliant disciple of Favre, who labored so long and unweariedly in Germany; St. Aloysius Gonzaga and St. Stanislaus Kostka, two young saints whose beautiful lives have been an inspiration to many of their own age; St. Edmund Campion, our famous English martyr, beloved by all, whose brilliant talents won the admiration of Queen Elizabeth, who was later to sign his death warrant; St. John Ogilvie, the gallant Scotch martyr, whose last word on the way to his cruel death was a blessing in exchange for a curse; St. Peter Claver, the slave of the slaves, who passed his life ministering to the wants of the Negroes amid the filth and disease of the slave ships; Blessed Charles Spinola, missionary to Japan, exposed for three years to the scorching rays of the sun in a wooden cage in company with twenty or thirty other prisoners, and then burnt alive; St. John de Britto, tracked by the Brahmins through the forests of India like a wild beast and at last taken prisoner and beheaded, after having converted whole districts to Christ; St. Francis Regis, zealous lover of souls and unwearied laborer in his Lord's vineyard; St. Claude de la Colombière, chaplain of the beautiful and unfortunate Queen of James II and promoter of the devotion to the Sacred Heart; Père de Ravignan, who by his preaching brought the young men of France from the unbelief that followed in the wake of the Revolution to the Faith of Christ—these are but a few of the noble and illustrious names on the roll of the Society.

And what of

> All the unnumbered rank and file
> Of God's own soldiery

—those whose labors have been none the less blessed because hidden, whose merits are known to God alone?

From his place in Heaven, Ignatius, the soldier Saint of Christ, looking down upon his army, sees its trials, its sufferings, its triumphs and its labors, and surely says—

"Well done!"

If you have enjoyed this book, consider making your next selection from among the following . . .

St. Catherine of Siena. *F. A. Forbes*. 6.00
St. Ignatius of Loyola. *F. A. Forbes*. 6.00
St. Teresa of Avila. *F. A. Forbes*. 6.00
St. Athanasius. *F. A. Forbes*. 6.00
St. Vincent de Paul. *F. A. Forbes* 6.00
St. Monica. *F. A. Forbes*. 6.00
Pope St. Pius X. *F. A. Forbes* 8.00
The Guardian Angels 2.00
Eucharistic Miracles. *Joan Carroll Cruz* 15.00
The Incorruptibles. *Joan Carroll Cruz* 13.50
Padre Pio—The Stigmatist. *Fr. Charles Carty* 15.00
Ven. Francisco Marto of Fatima. *Cirrincione,* comp.. . . . 1.50
The Facts About Luther. *Msgr. P. O'Hare* 16.50
Little Catechism of the Curé of Ars. *St. John Vianney* . . 6.00
The Curé of Ars—Patron St. of Parish Priests. *O'Brien*. . 5.50
The Four Last Things: Death, Judgment, Hell, Heaven . . 7.00
Confession of a Roman Catholic. *Paul Whitcomb*. 1.50
The Catholic Church Has the Answer. *Paul Whitcomb*. . . 1.50
The Sinner's Guide. *Ven. Louis of Granada* 12.00
True Devotion to Mary. *St. Louis De Montfort* 8.00
Autobiography of St. Anthony Mary Claret 13.00
I Wait for You. *Sr. Josefa Menendez* 75
Little Lives of the Great Saints. *John O'Kane Murray* . . 18.00
Prayer—The Key to Salvation. *Fr. Michael Müller* 7.50
The Victories of the Martyrs. *St. Alphonsus Liguori* 10.00
Canons and Decrees of the Council of Trent. *Schroeder* . 15.00
Sermons of St. Alphonsus Liguori for Every Sunday . . . 16.50
A Catechism of Modernism. *Fr. J. B. Lemius* 5.00
Alexandrina—The Agony and the Glory. *Johnston* 6.00
Abortion: Yes or No? *Dr. John L. Grady, M.D.*. 2.00
Hell Quizzes. *Radio Replies Press*. 1.50
Purgatory Quizzes. *Radio Replies Press* 1.50
Virgin and Statue Worship Quizzes. *Radio Replies Press* . 1.50
The Holy Eucharist. *St. Alphonsus*. 10.00
Meditation Prayer on Mary Immaculate. *Padre Pio* 1.50
Little Book of the Work of Infinite Love. *de la Touche*. . 3.00
Textual Concordance of/Holy Scriptures. *Williams.* H.B. . 35.00
Douay-Rheims Bible. *Leatherbound* 35.00
The Way of Divine Love. (pocket, unabr.). *Menendez* . . . 8.50
Prices subject to change.

The Secret of Mary. *St. Louis De Montfort* 5.00
St. Maria Goretti. *Fr. Poage, C. P.* 6.00
Stories of Padre Pio. *Tangari* 8.00
Miraculous Images of Our Lady. *Joan Carroll Cruz* 20.00
Miraculous Images of Our Lord. *Cruz* 13.50
Brief Catechism for Adults. *Fr. Cogan* 9.00
Raised from the Dead. *Fr. Hebert* 16.50
Autobiography of St. Margaret Mary 5.00
Thoughts and Sayings of St. Margaret Mary 5.00
The Voice of the Saints. *Comp. by Francis Johnston* . . . 7.00
The 12 Steps to Holiness and Salvation. *St. Alphonsus* . . 7.50
The Rosary and the Crisis of Faith. *Cirrincione/Nelson* . . 2.00
Sin and Its Consequences. *Cardinal Manning* 6.00
Fourfold Sovereignty of God. *Cardinal Manning* 5.00
Dialogue of St. Catherine of Siena. *Transl. Thorold* 10.00
Catholic Answer to Jehovah's Witnesses. *D'Angelo* 12.00
Twelve Promises of the Sacred Heart. (100 cards) 5.00
Life of St. Aloysius Gonzaga. *Fr. Meschler* 12.00
The Love of Mary. *D. Roberto* 8.00
Begone Satan. *Fr. Vogl* 3.00
The Prophets and Our Times. *Fr. R. G. Culleton* 13.50
St. Therese, The Little Flower. *John Beevers* 6.00
Mary, The Second Eve. *Cardinal Newman* 3.00
Devotion to Infant Jesus of Prague. *Booklet* 75
The Wonder of Guadalupe. *Francis Johnston* 7.50
Apologetics. *Msgr. Paul Glenn* 10.00
Baltimore Catechism No. 1 . . . . 3.50
Baltimore Catechism No. 2 . . . . 4.50
Baltimore Catechism No. 3 . . . . 8.00
An Explanation of the Baltimore Catechism. *Kinkead* . . . 16.50
Bible History. *Schuster* 13.50
Blessed Eucharist. *Fr. Mueller* 9.00
Catholic Catechism. *Fr. Faerber* 7.00
The Devil. *Fr. Delaporte* 6.00
Evidence of Satan in the Modern World. *Cristiani* 10.00
Fifteen Promises of Mary. (100 cards) 5.00
Life of Anne Catherine Emmerich. 2 vols. *Schmoeger* . . . 37.50
Life of the Blessed Virgin Mary. *Emmerich* 16.50
Prayer to St. Michael. (100 leaflets) 5.00
Prayerbook of Favorite Litanies. *Fr. Hebert* 10.00
Purgatory Explained. *Schouppe* 13.50
Purgatory Explained. (pocket, unabr.). *Schouppe* 9.00
Trustful Surrender to Divine Providence. *Bl. Claude* 5.00
Prices subject to change.

Forty Dreams of St. John Bosco. *Bosco* 12.50
Blessed Miguel Pro. *Ball* 6.00
Soul Sanctified. *Anonymous* 9.00
Wife, Mother and Mystic. *Bessieres* 8.00
The Agony of Jesus. *Padre Pio*. 2.00
Catholic Home Schooling. *Mary Kay Clark* 18.00
The Cath. Religion—Illus. & Expl. *Msgr. Burbach* 9.00
Wonders of the Holy Name. *Fr. O'Sullivan* 1.50
How Christ Said the First Mass. *Fr. Meagher* 18.50
Too Busy for God? Think Again! *D'Angelo* 5.00
St. Bernadette Soubirous. *Trochu* 18.50
Passion and Death of Jesus Christ. *Liguori* 10.00
Life Everlasting. *Garrigou-Lagrange* 13.50
Confession Quizzes. *Radio Replies Press* 1.50
St. Philip Neri. *Fr. V. J. Matthews* 5.50
St. Louise de Marillac. *Sr. Vincent Regnault* 6.00
The Old World and America. *Rev. Philip Furlong* 18.00
Prophecy for Today. *Edward Connor* 5.50
Bethlehem. *Fr. Faber* 18.00
The Book of Infinite Love. *Mother de la Touche*. 5.00
The Church Teaches. *Church Documents* 16.50
Conversation with Christ. *Peter T. Rohrbach*. 10.00
Purgatory and Heaven. *J. P. Arendzen*. 5.00
Liberalism Is a Sin. *Sarda y Salvany* 7.50
Spiritual Legacy/Sr. Mary of Trinity. *van den Broek* 10.00
The Creator and the Creature. *Fr. Frederick Faber* 16.50
Radio Replies. 3 Vols. *Frs. Rumble and Carty* 42.00
Convert's Catechism of Catholic Doctrine. *Geiermann*. . . 3.00
Incarnation, Birth, Infancy of Jesus Christ. *Liguori* 10.00
Light and Peace. *Fr. R. P. Quadrupani* 7.00
Dogmatic Canons & Decrees of Trent, Vat. I 9.50
The Evolution Hoax Exposed. *A. N. Field* 7.50
The Priest, the Man of God. *St. Joseph Cafasso* 13.50
Christ Denied. *Fr. Paul Wickens* 2.50
A Tour of the Summa. *Msgr. Paul Glenn* 18.00
Spiritual Conferences. *Fr. Frederick Faber* 15.00
Bible Quizzes. *Radio Replies Press* 1.50
Marriage Quizzes. *Radio Replies Press* 1.50
True Church Quizzes. *Radio Replies Press*. 1.50
Mary, Mother of the Church. *Church Documents* 4.00
The Sacred Heart and the Priesthood. *de la Touche* 9.00
Blessed Sacrament. *Fr. Faber* 18.50
Revelations of St. Bridget. *St. Bridget of Sweden* 3.00

Prices subject to change.

Story of a Soul. *St. Therese of Lisieux* 8.00
Catholic Children's Treasure Box Books 1-10 . . . . 35.00
Prayers and Heavenly Promises. *Cruz* 5.00
Magnificent Prayers. *St. Bridget of Sweden* 2.00
The Happiness of Heaven. *Fr. J. Boudreau* 8.00
The Glories of Mary. *St. Alphonsus Liguori* 16.50
The Glories of Mary. (pocket, unabr.). *St. Alphonsus* . . . 10.00
The Curé D'Ars. *Abbé Francis Trochu* 21.50
Humility of Heart. *Fr. Cajetan da Bergamo* 8.50
Love, Peace and Joy. (St. Gertrude). *Prévot* 7.00
Père Lamy. *Biver* 12.00
Passion of Jesus & Its Hidden Meaning. *Groenings* 15.00
Mother of God & Her Glorious Feasts. *Fr. O'Laverty* . . . 10.00
Song of Songs—A Mystical Exposition. *Fr. Arintero* . . . 20.00
Love and Service of God, Infinite Love. *de la Touche* . . 12.50
Life & Work of Mother Louise Marg. *Fr. O'Connell*. . . . 12.50
Martyrs of the Coliseum. *O'Reilly* 18.50
Rhine Flows into the Tiber. *Fr. Wiltgen*. 15.00
What Catholics Believe. *Fr. Lawrence Lovasik* 5.00
Who Is Therese Neumann? *Fr. Charles Carty* 2.00
Summa of the Christian Life. 3 Vols. *Granada* 36.00
St. Francis of Paola. *Simi and Segreti*. 8.00
The Rosary in Action. *John Johnson* 9.00
Is It a Saint's Name? *Fr. William Dunne* 2.50
St. Martin de Porres. *Giuliana Cavallini* 12.50
Douay-Rheims New Testament. *Paperbound* 15.00
St. Catherine of Siena. *Alice Curtayne* 13.50
Blessed Virgin Mary. *Liguori* 4.50
Chats With Converts. *Fr. M. D. Forrest* 10.00
The Stigmata and Modern Science. *Fr. Charles Carty* . . . 1.50
St. Gertrude the Great 1.50
Thirty Favorite Novenas 75
Brief Life of Christ. *Fr. Rumble* 2.00
Catechism of Mental Prayer. *Msgr. Simler* 2.00
On Freemasonry. *Pope Leo XIII* 1.50
Thoughts of the Curé D'Ars. *St. John Vianney* 2.00
Incredible Creed of Jehovah Witnesses. *Fr. Rumble* 1.50
St. Pius V—His Life, Times, Miracles. *Anderson*. 5.00
St. Dominic's Family. *Sr. Mary Jean Dorcy* 24.00
St. Rose of Lima. *Sr. Alphonsus* 15.00
Latin Grammar. *Scanlon & Scanlon* 16.50
Second Latin. *Scanlon & Scanlon* 12.00
St. Joseph of Copertino. *Pastrovicchi* 6.00

Prices subject to change.

Religious Customs in/Family. *Fr. Weiser, S. J.* 8.00
Mama! Why Did You Kill Us?. *Mondrone.* 2.00
St. Maximilian Kolbe—Knight of/Immaculata. *Smith* 6.00
Saint Michael and the Angels. *Approved Sources.* 7.00
Dolorous Passion of Our Lord. *Anne C. Emmerich.* 16.50
Our Lady of Fatima's Peace Plan from Heaven. *Booklet* . .75
Three Ways of the Spiritual Life. *Garrigou-Lagrange* . . . 6.00
Mystical Evolution. 2 Vols. *Fr. Arintero, O.P.* 36.00
St. Catherine Labouré of the Mirac. Medal. *Fr. Dirvin* . . 13.50
Manual of Practical Devotion to St. Joseph. *Patrignani* . . 15.00
The Active Catholic. *Fr. Palau* 7.00
Ven. Jacinta Marto of Fatima. *Cirrincione* 2.00
Reign of Christ the King. *Davies* 1.25
St. Teresa of Avila. *William Thomas Walsh* 21.50
Isabella of Spain—The Last Crusader. *Wm. T. Walsh* . . . 20.00
Characters of the Inquisition. *Wm. T. Walsh* 15.00
Philip II. *William Thomas Walsh.* H.B. 37.50
Blood-Drenched Altars—Cath. Comment. Hist. Mexico . . 20.00
Self-Abandonment to Divine Providence. *de Caussade* . . 18.00
Way of the Cross. *Liguorian* 1.00
Way of the Cross. *Franciscan* 1.00
Modern Saints—Their Lives & Faces, Bk. 1. *Ann Ball* . . 18.00
Modern Saints—Their Lives & Faces, Bk. 2. *Ann Ball.* . . 20.00
Divine Favors Granted to St. Joseph. *Pere Binet* 5.00
St. Joseph Cafasso—Priest of the Gallows. *St. J. Bosco* . 5.00
Catechism of the Council of Trent. *McHugh/Callan* 24.00
Why Squander Illness? *Frs. Rumble & Carty* 2.50
Fatima—The Great Sign. *Francis Johnston.* 8.00
Heliotropium—Conformity of Human Will to Divine. . . . 13.00
Charity for the Suffering Souls. *Fr. John Nageleisen* . . . 16.50
Devotion to the Sacred Heart of Jesus. *Verheylezoon* . . . 15.00
Fundamentals of Catholic Dogma. *Ott* 21.00
Litany of the Blessed Virgin Mary. (100 cards) 5.00
Who Is Padre Pio? *Radio Replies Press* 2.00
The Life of Christ. 4 Vols. H.B. *Anne C. Emmerich.* . . . 60.00
St. Anthony—The Wonder Worker of Padua. *Stoddard* . . 5.00
The Precious Blood. *Fr. Faber* 13.50
The Holy Shroud & Four Visions. *Fr. O'Connell* 2.00
Clean Love in Courtship. *Fr. Lawrence Lovasik.* 2.50
The Secret of the Rosary. *St. Louis De Montfort* 3.00

***At your Bookdealer or direct from the Publisher.
Call Toll Free 1-800-437-5876***

ABOUT THE AUTHOR

This book was authored by Mother Frances Alice Monica Forbes, a sister of the Society of the Sacred Heart, Scotland.

The future author was born on March 16, 1869 and was named Alice Forbes. Alice's mother died when she was a child, and her father became the dominant influence in her life, helping to form Alice's virile personality and great capacity for work. She was raised as a Presbyterian.

In 1900 Alice became a Catholic. The Real Presence in the Eucharist had been the big stumbling-block to her conversion, but one day she was hit by the literal truth of Our Lord's words: "This is My Body." Only a few months after her conversion, she entered the Society of the Sacred Heart, becoming a 31-year-old postulant. She seems to have received her vocation at her First Communion, when Our Lord kindled in her heart "the flame of an only love."

In the convent, Sister Forbes used her keen intelligence and strong will to make generously and completely the sacrifices that Our Lord asked of her each day. She put great store by the virtue of obedience. Much of the latter part of her life was spent in illness and suffering, yet she was always kind and uncomplaining—a charming person and a "gallant" soul. Throughout her sufferings the most important thing to her was the love of God. She died in 1936.

Mother Frances Alice Monica Forbes wrote many

books, including a series of interesting short lives of selected Saints called "Standard Bearers of the Faith." One of these books, that on Pope St. Pius X, was very highly regarded by Cardinal Merry del Val, who was a close friend of Pope Pius X.

Other works by Mother Frances Alice Monica Forbes include *St. Ignatius Loyola, St. John Bosco: Friend of Youth, St. Teresa, St. Columba, St. Monica, St. Athanasius, St. Catherine of Siena, St. Benedict, St. Hugh of Lincoln, The Gripfast Series of English Readers* and *The Gripfast Series of History Readers*, various plays, and a number of other books.

The above information is from the book *Mother F. A. Forbes: Religious of the Sacred Heart—Letters and Short Memoir*, by G. L. Sheil (London: The Catholic Book Club, 1948, by arrangement with Longmans, Green & Co., Ltd.).